HOSEA
The Heart and Holiness of
GOD

BY

G. CAMPBELL MORGAN

Wipf and Stock Publishers
150 West Broadway • Eugene OR 97401

1998

Hosea: The Heart and Holiness of God

ISBN: 1-57910-169-0

Printed by *Wipf and Stock Publishers* 1998
150 West Broadway • Eugene OR 97401

CONTENTS

HOSEA : THE HEART AND HOLINESS OF GOD

I

THE PROPHET'S STORY

Hosea i.–ii. 1

" When Jehovah spake at the first by Hosea, Jehovah said unto Hosea, Go, take unto thee a wife of whoredom and children of whoredom ; for the land doth commit great whoredom, departing from Jehovah."—Hosea i. 2.

I am not proposing in these lectures anything in the nature of a full exposition of this marvellous prophecy. I propose rather to consider some of its essential light —light for all days and for all life. By way of introduction it may be well to remember some of the facts concerning it. Accepting the dating of the first verse, Hosea was evidently a prophet to the northern kingdom of Israel, not to the southern kingdom of Judah. The dates of the kings referred to cover a period of no less than one hundred and twenty-eight years. Which, of course, does not mean that he was prophesying for one hundred and twenty-eight years, but he must have exercised his ministry for at least seventy years. In this book we have not a full account of his preaching. Unquestionably he, or some one else—most likely himself—did, towards the end of that wonderful period of prophesying, commit to writing the general movement of his ministry. It reveals the conditions in the midst of which he preached, and gives us the salient points of that marvellous ministry.

The book is peculiar in one regard. Among these twelve prophets, which we commonly call Minor, there are three which are distinctively narrative prophecies. Two in themselves are stories : the Book of Jonah is a story with a prophetic value ; and so also is the Book of Habakkuk. Hosea is not in itself a story, but behind it there is a story, which emerges incidentally, and we find that the story gives colour to the ministry of Hosea.

It was the darkest period in all Israel's history. The prophet spoke to that nation as it passed down the swift decline to captivity. The story is that of tragedy in the prophet's domestic life, which coloured all his messages.

The words of the second verse of the first chapter refer to that tragedy, and reveal its influence on Hosea's ministry, and its value to him as a prophet of God. Let us first consider the story in itself ; then let us consider the story in the light of these words ; and finally let us attempt to gather up some of the values of the story for ourselves.

What is the story ?   Hosea married a woman named Gomer. As the result of the marriage three children were born to them—Jezreel, Lo-ruhamah, and Lo-ammi, naming them as they were named.   Then Gomer played him false, and he cast her out judicially, as she had left him in infidelity. After a while, when she had descended to the uttermost depths of degradation, having become merely a slave, the property of some one else, Hosea sought her out in her degradation, bought her at the price of a slave, and restored her to his side as his bride.

That is the story bluntly told. The first part is tragic, but it is not uncommon. The second part is by no means common, and is absolutely amazing. With the first part we are familiar : it is tragic, heart-breaking, but not unknown. But the story of a man seeking a woman when she has passed through all the period of passion, and has lost her value on the material level, and is merely a slave ; and of such a man, going after her, buying her for thirty shekels and bringing her back, and restoring her to his side as his bride, is something very uncommon. That is the domestic story that lies behind this prophecy.

Now we come to the statement of this verse ; " When Jehovah spake at the first by Hosea, Jehovah said unto Hosea, Go, take unto thee a wife of whoredom and children of whoredom ; for the land doth commit great whoredom, departing from Jehovah."

The statement in the form in which it is made has created a difficulty in the minds of many, and I recognize the reason for that sense of difficulty. I admit the strangeness of it, but submit that it is rather in the way the thing is said, than in what is really said.

It may appear, from our reading of it in our English translations, and, indeed, in the Hebrew Bible also, that Hosea states that he deliberately married a woman of sin, and that he did so at the command of Jehovah. But that is not so.

In the Revised Versions, both English and American,

by the side of the words, "When Jehovah spake at
the first by Hosea," there is a marginal note, and the
marginal note says, "or with." That is a slight
alteration, but the revisers evidently admitted Ewald's
view as possibly correct. I adopt it resolutely. It
gives us the true sense. "When Jehovah spake at
the first *with* Hosea." That refers not to Hosea's
preaching, but to his communion with God. That
antedates the prophetic work of Hosea.

Then notice very carefully that little phrase, "at
the first." The writer was looking back, from the
end of his ministry, when he was writing out his notes,
committing them to manuscript form, and he said in
effect : When away back there my ministry began,
when, before the tragedy came into my life, Jehovah
spoke with me, it was He Who commanded me to
marry Gomer. The statement distinctly calls her a
woman of whoredom, but it does not tell us that she
was that at the time. It certainly does mean that
God knew the possibilities in the heart of Gomer, and
that presently they would be manifested in her conduct,
and knowing, He commanded Hosea to marry her,
knowing also what his experience would do for him in
his prophetic work. When Hosea married Gomer, she
was not openly a sinning woman, and the children
antedated her infidelity. The earlier life of the
prophet was in all likelihood one of joy and happiness.

Israel at the time was playing the harlot from God,
and as Hosea's children were born, they were named,
and their naming reflected the age : Jezreel, telling of
coming judgment ; Lo-ruhamah, people that are not
obtaining mercy ; Lo-ammi, people that are rejected.
The domestic scene at first is the scene of peace and

quietness and blessedness ; but it reflects, in the naming of the children, the national condition.

Thus we discover the force of the statement. Hosea looked back over his own life, to the tragedy that had come to him. He might have said without any hesitation, That marriage was the mistake of my life. See the misery that has come to me through it. See the blight upon my children as a consequence of it. See the tragedy of the woman herself. If he had been interpreting along the line of the natural, that is how he would have referred to the circumstance. But in looking back he rose to the height of supernatural interpretation. He says, No, that is not so. God guided me. He said, Go thou, and take a wife ; and when He said it, being God, He knew all that was coming, and yet He said it.

With what result ? The result of the tragedy in his life was that he, Hosea, came to understand the heart of God, and what God suffered when His people sinned. He was admitted, through the mystery of his own tragedy, into an apprehension of what the sin of the nation meant against the heart of God. Hosea has been described as the prophet of the broken heart. The pain and agony of the man's heart is everywhere apparent, but it had become to him an interpretation of the agony of the heart of God. In his own experience he discovered what infidelity means to love ; and so, that the infidelity of Israel roused, not the wrath of God, though He was compelled by it to act in judgment, but the heart-break of God.

It is startling. I am not quite sure that we have grasped it even in our Christian thinking. Yet Calvary is the ultimate exposition of the tremendous fact. Hosea, in this communion with God, came to understand the sin of the nation as he could never have understood it apart from the experience of his own agony. It is so easy for us to speak of the love of God, and sometimes so difficult for us to understand that to postulate love accurately, is to postulate the possibility of suffering and agony. He learned what God suffered in the dark hours when he was alone. The infidelity of Gomer interpreted to Hosea the infidelity of Israel. God had said, " I have betrothed thee unto Me for ever." If he had preached without this experience, his prophesying would probably have been very different. The national sin might have roused his anger when he had described what it meant to God, but it produced a much deeper note. So, looking back, he said, God over-ruled this. He knew that through it I should pass. He knew what would happen to this woman, and yet He guided me. By that guidance I have come to understand the suffering of God.

Now what are the lessons which we are to learn from this story ? I think that the first is that God interprets Himself to us through our own experiences. Over and over again we find that the experiences of an hour cannot be understood at the time ; but presently we look back and see, that when we talked to Jehovah at the first, He led us, even though the thing we did brought us into tragedy, for in the midst of the tragedy we have discovered God.

It was so with Joseph. On the day when his brethren came and he made himself known to them, and when they were weeping and bewailing the fact that they had treated him so badly, Joseph said to them, " God did send me before you, to preserve life."

He said in effect, You treated me badly. You put me in the den. You sold me into slavery. Oh yes, you did it, but there is a higher realm of interpretation. I have suffered years of imprisonment. But now I see the meaning of it all: God sent me before you, to preserve life.

That is the final value of the story of Job. Is there anything grander in literature than those cycles of debate between Job and the great philosophers, who, nevertheless, could not account for him when he did not fit into their philosophy, and so rejected him. All the while God said, " My servant Job, a perfect and upright man." When we get to the end of the story, we find Job talking, and he has found God, and found God's meaning. The revelation of the story is that suffering cannot be accounted for at the moment. God may be preparing us for co-operation with Him, and doing something in our lives, the witness of which shall pass down the ages, to give the lie to a false philosophy of life.

When Jehovah spake at the first, it was God that guided Hosea. God interprets Himself to us through our own experiences. In the case of Hosea his own broken heart gave him an understanding of the heart of God ; and presently when, obedient to the command of God, he sought out and went to find Gomer, and found her degraded, and brought her back, he found God's attitude, even to those who by sin broke His heart. Thus the backward look reveals Divine guidance oftentimes when it seems most unlikely.

We have in the Book of Hosea one of the most arresting revelations of the real nature of sin, and one of the clearest interpretations of the strength of the Divine love.

No one can read the story of Hosea without realizing the agony of his heart. Then, lift the human to the level of the Infinite, and know this, that sin wounds the heart of God. I believe that the meaning of David when in his great penitential Psalm he said, " Against Thee, Thee only have I sinned." Some one says —Was that true ? Had he not sinned *against* Bathsheba ? No, he sinned *with* Bathsheba. His sin against Uriah, too, was in the last analysis sin against God. His sin was of that nature that caused pain to the heart of God, and wounded love.

There was a theologian in England some years ago who wrote a book of which the title was, *The Impassive God*, in which he sought to prove that God is incapable of real suffering. Well, that God is not my God. That is not the God revealed here. Sin breaks in upon the Divine order, ruins the rhythmic nature of the universe. Yes, but that is not its chief heinousness. Get into Hosea's soul when Gomer played him false and left him. That is how God feels, and that is what Hosea learned.

And we learn the strength of love. To that we will come back in a subsequent meditation. But one cannot close without reference to it. Chapter one in this book should include chapter two and the first verse. At the close of chapter one, at the ninth verse we read, " Call his name Lo-ammi ; for ye are not My people, and I will not be your God." Terrible words. But read on : " Yet the number of the children of Israel shall be as the sand of the sea, which cannot be measured nor numbered ; and it shall come to pass that, in the place where it was said unto them, Ye are not My people "—Lo-ruhamah—" it shall be said unto them, Ye are the sons of the living God. And the children of Judah and the children of Israel shall be gathered together, and they shall appoint themselves one head, and shall go up from the land ; for great shall be the day of Jezreel. Say unto your brethren, Ammi, and to your sisters, Ruhamah." God said Lo-ruhamah, Lo-ammi ; no mercy, a rejected people. Yes, but He said that is not all, that is not the last word. The Divine purpose will be fulfilled, and the day will come when you will say Ruhamah, mercy obtained ; Ammi, My people.

Hosea was in the mind of Peter when he wrote, " Who in time past were no people (that is, Lo-Ammi), but now are the people of God (that is, Ammi) ; who had not obtained mercy (that is, Lo-ruhamah) but now have obtained mercy (that is, Ruhamah)."

God suffers in the presence of sin ; but His love is such that presently, in spite of it all, He will find a way for the sinner to come home, a way of release, a way of ransom, a way of rescue.

II

THE DOOR OF HOPE

Hosea ii. 2–iii.

"The valley of Achor for a door of hope."—
Hosea ii. 15.

In this section we have a very remarkable merging of the prophet's experience, with its influence on his understanding of the sin of his people. We began reading at the second verse, "Contend with your mother, contend ; for she is not my wife, neither am I her husband." That is not the language of Hosea to his children about Gomer. That is the language of God concerning the nation. Here the prophet was delivering a message to the nation of Israel from God, but his language was the result of the bitterness of his own heart, and the sorrows through which he had passed. In his disowning of Gomer, and casting her out, there had been perfect agreement with the severity of God towards His people.

But now a new note emerges. Suddenly, from the language of severity, we pass to the language of a strange tenderness. Listen to some sentences : " I will allure her, and bring her into the wilderness, and speak to her heart " . . . " I will give her her vineyards from thence, and the valley of troubling for a door of hope ; and she shall make answer there, as in the days of her youth " . . . " Thou shalt call Me Ishi (that is, my husband—correlative of wife) . . . no longer Baali (that is, my master—the correlative of mistress) " . . . " I will betroth thee unto Me for ever." That is the new note. So far Hosea had learned the suffering of God through his own suffering. So far Hosea had learned the necessity and the inevitableness of the severity of God through his own relationship with Gomer. But now there is a new note, the note of restoration. Presently he will be commanded to action which will interpret this in his own experience.

We have then two matters to consider : First, the revelation of God ; and, secondly, its interpretation to Hosea.

The revelation of God is found in the words, " The valley of Achor for a door of hope." There, two ideas are placed in close connection, and declared to be inter-related, which we would hardly have thought of putting together. What are they ? Troubling, and hope.

We do not often talk about those two things together, except that sometimes we say that, in spite of the trouble, we are hoping for the best. That " in spite of the trouble " recognizes a conflict between trouble and hope. Hope means expectation that we shall escape from trouble. The declaration here relates them to each other. The troubling is the reason of hope, " The valley of troubling for a door of hope."

It is this connection between troubling and hope which reveals God. It is the relation between Law and Grace. Law creates troubling as the result of sin. Grace creates hope through the troubling. Let us consider the ideas in separation.

First, the valley of Achor, that is of troubling. Three times we find that phrase, " the valley of Achor," in the Bible. First, in the Book of Joshua, in connection with the story of Achan. And, by the way, observe the relationship between the words Achan and Achor. That relationship is not a mere coincidence. Achan means trouble, and Achor means troubling. It was so that the valley gained its name (Josh. vii. 26). It was there that judgment swift and terrible fell upon a man who had troubled the whole nation by compromising with evil things, and disobeying God.

The second occasion of its occurrence is in Isaiah, who was contemporary with Hosea. He linked the valley of Achor with Sharon as a place of rest for those who seek Jehovah. Then finally we find it here in Hosea. The valley of swift judgment, the place of troubling. So it gained its name. The valley of Achor in conjunction with Sharon, a place of rest and of pasturage and of flocks, and of blessedness to those who have sought Jehovah. The valley of Achor, the Door of Hope. Troubling swinging open a door of hope ; troubling leading presently to the place of peace and the place of rest.

The great truth that we thus face is that of God's severity with sin. Troubling as the result of sin is inevitable. It is inevitable by the law of God. This whole universe is constituted so. Stanley Jones in his great book, *The Christ of Every Road*, says : " We do not break the laws of the universe, we break ourselves upon them." Stanley Jones is right. We

never break the laws of the universe. We break
ourselves on them, and that is troubling. The whole
universe is built so that no man can escape from that
sequence. Put your hand in the fire, and the pain is the
troubling, and you cannot escape from it. You have
not broken the law ; but you have broken your hand.
Law conditions heaven. Violated law creates hell.
Troubling is the inherent necessity of sin. The way
is hedged and hindered, the false lovers are lost, and
there is nothing ultimately but desolation. Remember those words of our Lord, " Wide is the gate,
and broad is the way that leadeth to destruction."
The root sense of that word " destruction " is narrow-
ness. " Strait is the gate and narrow is the way that
leadeth to life," and life is breadth. The way of sin
is easy, the gate is wide open, the highway is broad.
Yes, but watch it, watch it ; it is narrowing, until
life becomes crushed and cursed. That is always the
way of sin. The whole universe is built on that
pattern. The way of life is narrow ; yes, strait is
the gate. Stripping is needed to enter upon the way
of life. Narrow the way in the beginning, but mark
it, it broadens out into the spaciousness of life.

Thus we come to the note of Grace. The troubling
that comes in the wake of sin is the result of the
Divine government, and the Divine law, and the
Divine beneficence. If sin brought no penalty in its
track what would happen ? Utter destruction. The
troubling opens the door of hope. Because of it
presently Gomer will say, " I will return to my
husband." When he had spent all, and there arose a
mighty famine in the land, and the troubling came,
then the son said, " I will arise and go to my father " :

the door of hope for him. Desolation is the opportunity of remembering, and so the very disciplines
of God create for man the door of hope. " The valley
of Achor for a door of hope."

But it is the door of hope, and the figure suggests
responsibility. An open door is of no value unless I
pass through it. In the gloom and the darkness and
the misery that come to the soul through sin, the
soul is brought to the nakedness of personality, and
the sense of impoverishment. In my father's house
there are many hired servants, and I perish with
hunger. Yes, and the door of hope swings into the
light of the Father's home and the Father's heart, but
it is no use, unless we go through the door, no use unless
we reinforce the consciousness of the wrong that has
robbed and ruined us by return, " I will return to my
husband," " I will arise and go to my father."

Thus we reach the final stage in Hosea's training. So
far, he had learned the nature of sin as it wounds the
heart of God. He had agreed with the necessity for
severity with sin. Moreover, he had heard, in his
communion with God, the amazing statement that
the valley of Achor, the valley of troubling, is a door
of hope. At that point surely he was left wondering.
There was the tragedy in his own life, the infidelity of
Gomer, interpreting sin as infidelity to the God of
infinite love. Gomer had cut herself off from him,
and he judicially had been compelled to agree and
abandon her to her own choices, just as God had done.
The severity he understood, and agreed with as inevitable, because of sin. But here was something
new. He heard the amazing word, that the valley of
troubling was a door of hope. So far as the nature of

sin wounding the heart of God was concerned, that was an experience through which he had passed, and he understood it. So far as the severity that follows sin was concerned, that was an experience, and he understood it; but when he heard this word, that somehow through the troubling hope was created, he was in the presence of something of which he knew nothing in experience. Gomer was still away, Gomer was degraded, Gomer was suffering.

Now God broke in on his life with a command, a strange command, " Go again, love a woman beloved of her friend, and an adulteress." He was at once obedient; " So I bought her to me for fifteen pieces of silver, and a homer and a half of barley." That action must have run counter to all his natural feeling, but by obedience he learned another lesson about God, and was brought into a new experience of life.

What then was the interpretation of God that came to Hosea ? What have we seen of God in this book of the Old Testament ? I submit four things about God revealed in this prophecy. First, I find that God suffers when His people are unfaithful. I find, secondly, that God cannot tolerate or condone sin. I find, thirdly, that though that be so, God still loves the sinner, in spite of the sinner's sin. And I find, fourthly, that that being so, God seeks the sinner in order to restore him. These are the commonplaces of our Christian faith, and it is wonderful to see them gleaming and flashing on this Old Testament page.

First, God suffers when His people are unfaithful. When here I speak of " His people," I mean all people, for all are His. That truth finds explicit declaration in the prophecy of Ezekiel. " All souls are Mine."

When men are unfaithful to Him—God suffers. Faber uttered a profound truth when he sang,

> " There is no place where earth's sorrows
> Are felt more than up in heaven."

Has it ever occurred to you that there is no aggregate of human suffering except in God ?. I am in trouble, and you are in trouble, and another is in trouble— three people in trouble. But we cannot put the trouble of the three together, and say the result is three times the trouble of one. There is no aggregate of sorrow except in the heart of God. He feels my pain, thy pain, and his pain. All earth's sorrows are in the heart of God. Is there any sentence sublimer in all your Bible than the little sentence in our language, only three words, and all words of one syllable, " God is love." I always quarrel with the theologians when they tell me love is an attribute of God. It is no attribute. It is the sum totality of the attributes. As are the characteristics of a man to his character : so are the attributes to the love of God. He is love.

Creation was an act of love, and all law is an ex- pression of love. Love for ever suffers when the loved one suffers. I sometimes think that the difference between God's love and my love at its highest lies just there. I love, and if the one I love is untrue to me, I suffer. Why ? Because I have lost that love. God does not suffer in that way. He suffers because the one who ceases to love Him is suffering. There is an element of self in our love. There is none in God's. Jesus was on His way to the Cross. Weeping women were bewailing Him, and He said, " Women, daughters of Jerusalem, weep not for Me, but for yourselves and your children," showing the point and poignancy of His own agony. It was not that they were wronging Him, but that in wronging Him they were harming themselves. God suffers when His people are unfaithful. All the sin of humanity is causing suffering to God; the very suffering that man brings upon himself is most keenly felt in heaven.

But, secondly, I learn that God cannot tolerate or condone sin. Why not ? Always for the reason already given ; because sin is defeating the purpose of love, and entailing suffering. If you could persuade me that God could deal with sin lightly, you could by that argument prove to me He is no lover of the human soul. It is because sin reacts to blight and blast and dwarf and damn a man that God can make no terms with it. The reason for God's judgment of sin is that sin blasts and spoils those whom God loves.

And that leads to the third phase of interpretation. I learn from this prophecy that God still loves, in spite of sin. Many years ago a lad in a Sunday School class in England asked his Sunday School teacher : " Does God love naughty boys ? " and the teacher said, " No, certainly not." Oh, the unintentional blasphemy of telling a boy that ! If God did not love naughty boys, He never would have loved me ! Shakespeare says,

> " Love is not love,
> That alters when it alteration finds."

Where did Shakespeare learn that lesson ? He learned it nowhere except from the literature that reveals this God. God still loves, in spite of sin.

And so we come to the final revelation which is the

heart and core of the Gospel. He sent Hosea after
Gomer, and said, Do what I do. He seeks the sinner,
in order to restore.

> " Lord, Thou hast here Thy ninety-and-nine,
>   Are they not enough for Thee ?
> But the Shepherd made answer, This of Mine
>   Has wandered away from Me,
> And although the road be rough and steep,
>   I go to the desert to find My sheep."

He seeks the sinner He loves. He will make no terms
with sin. He loves in spite of sin. Then begins
Heaven's great movement, God's great emprise, the
quest for the sinner that has cut himself off from God.
Oh, the music of it as it comes down the centuries, and
sings its song in your heart, " God so loved the world."

Let us look at the method and value of this final stage
in the training of this prophet. God said, " Go again,
love a woman beloved of her friend, and an adulteress."
He did not say, " Go again, and restore her." That
was a sequence. He said, " Go again, and love her."
That brings us face to face with difficulty. We of
ourselves cannot do it ; and it is no use pretending
we can. Mark Twain in his book, *A Yankee at the
Court of King Arthur*, makes his Yankee determined
that the king should understand his people, and so
causes him to disguise himself and travel among the
downtrodden folk. The king does not know how to
behave on that level, and so addresses one of his
people as " Varlet." The Yankee at once tells him
he must not so address them, as he is brother to them
all. Then the king exclaims, " Brother, to dirt like
that ? " That is the human heart. Go, love a woman
who has ruined you, and an adulteress. Dirt like that !

I cannot do it in my own strength. If I ever do that it will be because something happens in me that makes me a different man altogether. Human nature is not equal to it.

It is a wonderful proof that Hosea was living in communion with God that he obeyed. The Eastern colour makes the picture vivid. Observe her condition when he found her. How much did he pay for her? Fifteen pieces of silver. The price of the slave was thirty pieces of silver. He paid half-price! This woman had sunk so low, that he picked her up at half-price! And notice again : " And a homer of barley, and a half-homer of barley." What was a homer and half of barley? Exactly the rations allowed to the slave for a day. So he got her for half-price and a day's ration.

And then what ? " And I said unto her, Thou shalt abide for me many days ; thou shalt not play the harlot, and thou shalt not be any man's wife ; so will I be unto thee." This was the discipline of deprivation of the false, and of the true, for a period. This in order to give her the time for revaluation, of thinking things through. But he brought her to himself, and he said to her, " So will I be also unto thee." While you are deprived, I am deprived also ; you living in separation, deprived of the false and true, I share the deprivation. That is the final word in the tender method of love.

And then what ? The whole prophecy is the answer. The notes that thrill and throb and tremble like a pæan of triumph to the end, show that Hosea entered into the highest experience of life and love.

" Rejoice with Me, I have found the sheep that was

lost." He entered into that. You cannot explain
that to the man of the world. I do not think Hosea
went after Gomer because he loved her, but because
God sent him. But I am perfectly sure that when he
went, the love came back.

I remember over thirty years ago at Northfield,
talking to my beloved friend, Dr. Scofield. He told me
a little story then that has lived with me ever since.
He was talking about the motive for Christian service,
and he and I were agreeing that the motive for Christian
service is love of God, love of Christ. " Lovest thou
Me," said Jesus to Simon. He did not say, Do you
love these people, but, Do you love Me ? In that
connection Dr. Scofield told me this story. When
he was pastor in Dallas, Texas, a girl, a member of his
Church, was going out to the Mission Field, and she
came to say good-bye to him before she left. He said
to her, " Well, lassie, I am so glad you love these Chinese
well enough to give your life to them." To which she
quickly replied, " Oh, Dr. Scofield, don't you make
any mistake. I don't love the Chinese. I have
absolutely no love for them. I rather dislike them."
He said, " Why then are you going ? " " Why am
I going ? Because I love my Lord, and He has told
me to go." After seven years she came back, on her
first furlough, and she came into the same study, and
said to him, " Dr. Scofield, do you remember what I
said to you in this room when I was going out to
China ? " " Yes," he said, " I very well remember."
She said, " I told you I did not love the Chinese a bit.
Dr. Scofield, I was telling you the truth, but I love
them now. I went because I loved my Lord, but now
I love them, and I did not even want to come home

on furlough." That is the principle. Go, love **a** woman. He went; he bought her; he put her in the place of deprivation, on the way to restoration; and by and by the love came. Thus he had touched God in the activity that seeks to save, and he had touched God in the deepest joy in his life.

In conclusion, let us make one or two general observations. First, sin has no door of hope, neither can the sinner open a door of hope. Only love can do it, only love. There is tremendous significance in that phrase of the New Testament, " Without God, and without hope in the world."

That word *troubling* needs an interpretation. I find it by turning from Hosea to John. There came an hour in the ministry of Jesus, when I hear Him saying, " Now is My soul troubled; and what shall I say ? Father, save Me from this hour. . . . Father, glorify Thy name." Then, in a moment or two, His voice is speaking again, " Now is the judgment of this world ; now shall the prince of this world be cast out. And I, if I be lifted up from the earth, will draw all men unto Myself." " Now is My soul troubled." Through the troubling of Another, to the uttermost bounds, the door of hope is open for me. The troubling that created the door of hope was not the troubling of Gomer or of Israel, but the troubling of God, and the broken heart of God. The sorrow of God swings open the door of hope. Thus grace in fellowship with law, agrees with the severity that must follow sin ; but catches it, bears it, banishes it, and opens the highway for the sinning soul back to the heart and the Home of God.

Finally observe the unveiling of God, and the revealing of consequent responsibility. As to the unveiling of God, there is only one thing to say. It is what you and I sing so often, " Love so amazing." God forgive us if we ever lose our amazement at the love of God.

> " I stand all amazed at the love Jesus offers me,
>   Oh, it was wonderful ! "
> " Amazing love, and can it be."

These are lines of hymns we sing,

> " Love so amazing,"—

Well, go on ; finish it—

> " so Divine,
> Demands my life, my soul, my all."

But this unveiling of God is also the revealing of responsibility. Apprehension of what God is, demands correspondence in us. " If a man say, I love God, and hateth his brother, he is a liar." If a man say he love his brother, and simply declares it in academic satisfaction, he is a traitor. This is of vital importance. Hosea, go after Gomer, and love her as I love this people. Carry out in your own relationship the things you have seen in *Me*. And as Hosea did it, he understood more perfectly the heart of God.

It is not enough to know that God is love. If we know it, He calls us to act in correspondence with that love in our dealings with men. That is where Jonah failed. Jonah did not want to go to Nineveh because he knew God so well. He knew perfectly well if he did go there and preach, and Nineveh repented, God would forgive. He knew God, and he knew God might forgive Nineveh, and he did not want Nineveh forgiven, and he did not want to go. But, thank God, for another word from Jonah, " The word of Jehovah came unto Jonah the second time." The word of Jehovah may be coming to some of us the second time. You have seen something of this God. Well, go, and love that derelict man, woman, somebody outside, somebody you can get for half-price and a day's rations ; go and love them, go and serve them ; go and buy them, go and gather them in. Go and pour your life out for some derelict ; and on the wings of your sacrifice you will rise into fellowship with God, as did Hosea.

III

JOINED TO IDOLS

Hosea iv.

" Ephraim is joined to idols ; let him alone."—
Hosea iv. 17.

The opening words of this chapter introduce the rest of the book. From here to the end we have a condensed account of the burden of the prophet's messages, lasting, as we have said before, according to the dating, for a long period of years. At least for seventy years Hosea was the preacher of righteousness in the northern kingdom of Israel.

This chapter in itself is a message to the whole nation. We may call it an indictment of the nation. The nation is portrayed in its terrible pollution. The cause of the pollution is clearly declared. " My people are destroyed for lack of knowledge." The result is described as that of the uttermost desolation, the judgment of God falling upon them, not as the stroke of a capricious Judge, but as the inevitable outworking and result of the fact that they had rejected knowledge, and so were perishing for the lack of it.

Now in this chapter these oft-quoted words are found, and our first business is to ask very simply and yet very definitely, what do they mean ? " Ephraim is joined to idols ; let him alone."

In answering that question I shall have to run counter to a popular and almost universal interpretation. The common interpretation has been that at this point in this chapter of judgment, God says that because Ephraim is joined to his idols, He will abandon him, He will let him alone. " Ephraim is joined to idols," therefore God says, I leave him. It is remarkable, the almost complete agreement of expositors at this point. Nevertheless they are wrong. Expositors have a habit, like sheep, of going in flocks, and sometimes it may be said of them, " All we like sheep have gone astray." It is certainly so here. That certainly is not the meaning of the words. God was not abandoning Ephraim. That would contradict the whole teaching of the prophet. That would contradict the truth already revealed, that of the valley of troubling as the door of hope. And that would contradict the great sigh and cry of God which emerges later on, " How shall I give thee up, Ephraim ? "

Therefore we ask again, what does it mean ? Let us note the context. Verses fifteen, seventeen, eighteen, and nineteen constitute a separate paragraph, which is part of the address, part of the message, and yet in some senses is separated from it. Hosea was a prophet to the northern kingdom of Israel. Israel was going rapidly down the steep declivity that led presently to exile. Judah, in the south, was more loyal to God than Israel, and at this point the prophet who was prophesying to Israel, as it were, flung a message across to Judah in the south. " Though thou, Israel, play the harlot, yet let not Judah offend." It was a word to Judah. " Come not ye unto Gilgal, neither go ye up to Beth-aven." Bethel was the house of God ; but the prophet with a fine satire does not call it Bethel, the house of God, but Beth-aven, the house of vanity. He said to Judah, " Do not go to Gilgal, neither go up to Beth-aven, nor swear, As Jehovah liveth." Still thus talking to Judah he said, " For Israel hath behaved himself stubbornly, like a stubborn heifer ; now will Jehovah feed them as a lamb in a large place. Ephraim "—that is Israel, the name of the dominant tribe, which he so constantly used—" Ephraim is joined to his idols ; let him alone."

It was not the statement that God would let Ephraim alone. It was a warning to Judah that she must let him alone " Ephraim is joined to idols ; let him alone." The prophet was warning Judah, that she enter into no alliance, either trade, or political, or military, with Israel. While Hosea was prophesying to the northern kingdom, his compatriot and fellow-prophet, Isaiah, was preaching in the southern kingdom, and he thus reinforced the messages of Isaiah with this brief word, " Ephraim is joined to idols ; let him alone." It was the word of the prophet to the loyal to have no complicity with the disloyal. It was the word of warning to those who were still in greater measure maintaining their right relationship with God, not to imperil their own safety by coming into any contact with Ephraim, " Ephraim is joined to idols ; let him alone."

While it is perfectly true that God does not abandon the disloyal, the loyal must not enter into alliance with the disloyal. Thus the message constitutes the emergence in this prophecy of a principle which runs through all the Biblical literature, and finds crystallized expression more than once, as you will remember, in the New Testament Scriptures. " Come ye out from among them, and be ye separate, saith the Lord, and touch no unclean thing. What concord hath Christ with Belial ? or what portion hath a believer with an unbeliever." It reveals the necessity of refraining from, and refusing complicity with evil, on the part of those who are standing for God.

Three matters then arrest our attention : First, the thing forbidden, idolatry ; secondly, the condition described, Ephraim joined to idols ; and thirdly, the warning uttered to Judah, " Let him alone."

In all the Old Testament Literature, and quite definitely in the New Testament, idolatry is viewed as an intolerable evil. It was the sin of Israel, the thing that cursed it, and blighted it, and blasted it. What then is idolatry ? I know that the question sounds almost absurd, for of course the thing is so familiar that we are all inclined to say that every one knows what idolatry is. But I am not sure that our thinking is always accurate or adequate on the subject. So I do ask—What is idolatry ? It certainly is a serious question, and we ought to face it.

Let me say first that idolatry is by no means dead. We sometimes speak of Britain and America as Christian countries. There is a sense in which such a description may be permissible, but in the full sense there is no Christian country. We are still saturated and cursed with idolatry.

What then is idolatry ? Let us first recognize that idolatry is pre-eminently religious. The idolater is not a man who has broken with religion. He is practising it. If a man is avowedly an atheist, and honestly so, then he cannot be an idolater. And yet in his case, however honest he may be in his claim to be an atheist, his whole life is mastered by some central devotion, which is his god, and so in the last analysis he also is an idolater. But in our general use of the word, it applies to those who themselves claim to be religious, or to have a religion. I repeat, the idolater is not the man who has broken with religion, but the one who is practising it. All the forms of idolatry, which exist where the Christian light has not broken, are religious. Every form under which man worships is a demonstration of his capacity for religion, and his attempt to realize and satisfy that capacity. This applies to those with which we are familiar in our reading of the Bible ; the worship of Baal, the worship of Moloch, and the worship of Mammon ; or those familiar to us in our reading of history, outside the Bible ; the worship of Zeus, of Diana, of Astarte, all of them. They are all religious. When Paul went to Athens, he saw the city full of idols. When he began to address the Stoics and Epicureans, on Mars Hill, he said, " I perceive that ye are "—not, very superstitious ; never was there a more unfortunate mistranslation than that, but—" I perceive that ye are very religious." Idolatry is religious.

Well, what are idols ? Let us first confine ourselves to the word as it occurs in our text : " Joined to idols." The word so translated simply means images. Quite literally the word, Atsab, means something carved. By use it means a carved representation of something else. Idolatry is the worship of an image, as the image is supposed to represent God—a god, if you like so to say. That is idolatry. Idolatry is the worship of false representations of God.

Let us consider this briefly in application to the history of the kingdom of Israel. When Solomon died, the popular voice was heard appealing against the burdens of taxation, and so forth, imposed upon the people by the king. As a king, Solomon was a ghastly failure. The period of Solomon's reign for forty years over the whole nation was very much like the sway of Lorenzo de' Medici in Florence. He held the people enthralled by magnificent display and artistic splendour, and songs and flowers, and the refined and the beautiful, and nearly crushed their life out by extortion. Savonarola was raised up and broke his power. Solomon's reign was like that, and when Solomon died, the voice of Jeroboam was heard speaking out on behalf of the oppressed people, asking Rehoboam, the son of Solomon, to lift their burdens. Rehoboam, the young fool, imagining that autocracy is hereditary, and taking counsel with some of the younger men, came back with the answer, " If my father chastised you with whips, I will chastise you with scorpions " ; then the cry went up, " To your your tents, O Israel," and the kingdom was rent in twain ; Israel in the north, Judah in the south. What then did Jeroboam do ? He did not advise the people to give up the worship of God. He felt the worship of God was vital ; but because, if they travelled down into Judah and Jerusalem for their great feasts and festivals, they would put in danger his political programme in the north, he said, We will have a system of our own. Consequently, for political reasons, he set up two centres for their worship, one was Bethel, and the other Gilgal, and he set up the two golden calves to be worshipped. He did not, however, call them to worship the calves, but God, as represented by the calves. That was the beginning of the idolatry of Israel. It ran on down the years, until all sorts of misrepresentations of God were brought in. But they were still worshipping. They would have told you they were worshipping God, but they were worshipping God falsely represented. That is idolatry ; it is religion seeking to worship God through any representation of Himself except that which has come to men by direct revelation. That is idolatry. That is the evil which includes within itself all misery, all disaster, all judgment ultimately.

I have already referred to Isaiah as contemporary with Hosea. In the southern kingdom of Judah, somewhere about the same time, he thundered against this attempt to represent God. Hear his words (Isa. xl. 18–22) :

> " To whom then will ye liken God ? or what likeness will ye compare unto Him ? The image, a workman hath cast it, and the goldsmith overlayeth it with gold, and casteth for it silver chains. He that is too impoverished for such an oblation chooseth a tree that will not rot ; he seeketh unto him a skilful workman to set up a graven image, that shall not be moved.
>
> " Have ye not known ? have ye not heard ? hath it not been told you from the beginning ? have ye not understood from the foundations of the earth ? It is He that sitteth above the circle of the earth, and the inhabitants thereof are as grasshoppers, that stretcheth out the heavens as a curtain, and spreadeth them out as a tent to dwell in."

" To whom then will ye liken Me ? " saith God. The prophet was showing the impossibility of representing God by any likeness. That is the sin forbidden in the Second Commandment, " Thou shalt not make unto thee a graven image, nor any likeness of anything that is in heaven above, or that is in the earth beneath, or that is in the water under the earth ; thou shalt not bow down thyself unto them, nor serve them."

All of which is based upon the recognition of the fact that no man can make a representation of God ; and that as surely as he do so, or attempt to do it, and then worship God through his own representation, he is worshipping God through a misrepresentation, which will react upon him for his own blasting. That is idolatry.

If man thinks of God, recognizes God, and then says, Now I must grasp God, and understand God, and I must have something that represents God to me, and proceeds to create that representation, he is attempting the impossible. Yet it is such an easy thing, a natural thing to do. Man says, Give me something at which I can look, something that will keep God before my eyes. Then if a man attempts to satisfy his own demand he can only do it in one way, and that is by projecting his own personality, or the personality of some other human being into infinitude. That is the history of all the great idolatries. Some lower forms of idolatry have deified animals, always with bestial results in the lives of the devotees. But when man projects himself into infinitude, and says God is an infinite human Being, then what he projects is an abortion, a monstrosity, a failure. The result is Zeus, the god of force ; Moloch, the god of brutal cruelty ; Baal, the god of lust and impurity. All idols which are representations of God, projected from the thinking of human personality, are necessarily misrepresentations of God, because man is in himself a failure.

Israel had taken the lower level in making calves represent God. They had rejected the true knowledge, with the result that they were filthy and polluted with sins which were animal in their nature.

Every form of religion which is based upon a denial of the God of revelation is idolatry. I am not now thinking about India, I am not thinking about China, I am not thinking about Africa. I am thinking about countries nominally Christian in so far as, in their thinking about God, they have turned from revelation.

But men must have some representation ; and God has given us the representation. In the fulness of time He came ; and in that most illuminative word of Paul, when writing about Jesus, He is " the Image of the invisible God." Idolatry to-day consists in an attempt to worship God while denying the finality of the unveiling of God that came in the personality of Jesus. If men merely treat Jesus as on the human level, and say, We will take His teaching, such as we agree with, and try and obey that, and work out our own salvation, they are idolaters. They are worshipping at the shrine of a false representation of God. And to-day, as always, such sin of the spirit reacts, and becomes presently the pollution of all life, individual, family, social, national. Trouble everywhere to-day is due to the fact that man is an idolater, that he is turning from the unveiling of God given in Christ.

Now let us examine the condition of Israel as

revealed in the words : " Joined to idols." " Joined "
is an arresting word. The primitive root means
simply joined, but in common use in the Hebrew
language, as revealed in other places in the Literature,
it was used in the sense of being held under, as by
a spell. It suggested being fascinated in an evil
sense ; to be held by the spell of idolatry. Israel is
drugged with its own pollutions, deluded by its false
idea of God ; and that at the first by its own choice,
until presently, more terrible yet, contentedly the
nation was seen by the prophet so drugged and deluded
by idolatry, linked up with it, held by it, satisfied with
it ; while all the time it was working its ruin—" joined
to idols."

To my own heart and soul, the supreme terror of
the present hour is that of the satisfaction of humanity
with false forms of religion, which satisfaction is issuing
in lust, and licence, and dethronement of God. Out
of it comes the declaration that there is no God who
cares, that we are the victims of our own personality,
or the victors, according to our own choices. Be-
haviourism, humanism, these are the denials of moral
responsibility. Observe the literature which is being
poured out upon our young people in defence of that
very view of life ; all coming from a false view of God,
all advanced in the name of religion. Volumes have
issued from the press which are utterly immoral in
their issue and influence, containing teaching which
cuts the nerve of morality, claims that there is no value
in the moral standards of the Church and the moral
standards of Jesus. Yet much of such literature
makes a gesture to God, patronizes God. The writers
of such books have lost the vision of the God of the

Bible, the God of holiness Who can make no compromise with evil, because He is the God of love. That is idolatry, and it is a terrible thing when it has to be said of any man or of a nation, it is joined to idols.

All of which brings us to, and gives force to the injunction of the prophet, " Ephraim is joined to idols ; *let him alone."* Which means, in the terms of our own time and our own thinking, Loyalty to God cannot compromise. God as He has been revealed is God alone, and there can be no compromise. Loyalty to Christ cannot co-operate with those who deny Him in any sense. To-day there is a tolerance abroad which is high treason. There is a passion saturating the air for a comprehension which sacrifices the very heart of the Christian religion, and the very core of the Gospel of the Nazarene. There is a widespread patronage of Jesus which consents to name Him as one among others, and to put Him into comparison. This is in itself a blank denial, and a subtle form of idolatry ; and this word of God has immediate application, " Ephraim is joined to his idols ; let him alone."

In 1893 there was held the World's Fair in Chicago ; and in connection therewith they had a great gathering for the study of comparative religion. That gathering did more harm upon the mission field than we have yet grasped. When we consented to sit down and compare Jesus with Buddha, Zoroaster, and others, we were compromising our message. He is out of the realm of comparison. Very different is the story of Stanley Jones. He has sat at round-table conferences with representatives of other religions. He invited teachers and leaders and poets of India to sit with him ;

but never for a moment did he consent to put Christ into comparison with others, except for showing the absolute supremacy and finality of Jesus. That is the difference.

A man must be true to his own conscience. I have been asked if I would not go to some meeting at which representatives of other religions were to speak— Mohammedan and Jewish. No. I will respect the Mohammedan, and I will respect the Jewish rabbi, but I cannot stand on a religious platform with them. They are joined to false representations of God. If some one says he is not sure about that, I shall reply, then he is not sure about Jesus Christ, not sure about His finality. So long as we are prepared to compare Him, we are something less than Christian. So long as we put Him into comparison with others, it is because we have not risen to the height of intellectual comprehension concerning Him, to say nothing of volitional surrender to Him. Until we see Him alone as " the Image of the invisible God," filling all the horizon to the uttermost bound, we have not really seen Him at all, and our relation to Him lacks the uttermost of devotion. The hour is coming, nay, the hour is here, when loyal souls ought at least to stand separate from all complicity with any form of the misrepresentation of God, even though the form be some new presentation of Jesus that denies the things of Revelation. There must be no compromise.

It may be objected that to insist upon that will be to thin the ranks of the Christian Church. So much the better for the enterprise of God in Christ. The Church to-day, alas, has passed under the blight of a passion for statistics. I tremble sometimes when some of my brethren tell me they have the largest Church membership in the city or the State. They are in danger ! I would like to be allowed to have the privilege of revising their Church rolls ! It would be of value to know how many of those enrolled really represent vital Christianity ! The sifting of the ranks oftentimes is the strengthening of a campaign. Ephraim is joined to his idols. Judah, the spell of idolatry is upon Israel. She is cursed, dazed, drugged. She is deluded, she is doomed. Judah, stand away ! No alliance with her ! Stand away, as you value your own soul ! " Come out from among them, and be ye separate."

Finally, let it be recognized that this call to separation does not include bitterness towards those from whom you separate ; but a great love and compassion and courtesy.

" Ephraim is joined to idols," Judah, " Let her alone." God is not going to let her alone. God is going to deal with her. We shall hear the cry of the Divine heart by and by, " How shall I give thee up, Ephraim ? " But so long as Ephraim gives God up, we are to have no complicity with her in her idolatry. The principle is of application individually. I cannot make it for you ; you cannot make it for me. But it is a clarion call to those who name the Name to stand clear of all complicity with false representations of God.

IV

THE DEPARTURE OF GOD

Hosea v.–vi. 3

" I will go and return to My place, till they acknowledge their offence, and seek My face ; in their affliction
they will seek Me earnestly."—Hosea v. 15.

JEHOVAH is the Speaker. " I will go and return to
My place, till they acknowledge their offence, and seek
My face ; in their affliction they will seek Me earnestly."
In this chapter the prophet's special message was
delivered to the priests, to the people, and to the king.
It was a national word to Israel, but through the
priests and the king, that is, the religious and the
civil rulers. Its burden was that of national pollution,
and consequent Divine judgment falling upon the
nation.

The background is that of intense gloom. Israel
is in rebellion against her God, and Judah is in danger.
It is to be observed that twice over he linked Judah
with Israel in what he had to say. In our previous
study we were considering the word to Judah, which
the prophet flung across the border-line between the
southern and the northern kingdom, when he warned
the southern nation against making any alliance with
Israel, as he said, " Ephraim is joined to idols ; let
him alone."

Quite evidently Judah was not obedient to the warning. She had been entering into league with Israel, and seeking help from Assyria. There was a political arrangement between the northern and southern kingdoms in an attempt to save them from what they supposed to be impending calamity. In this message, then, while specially first addressed to the northern kingdom, the prophet twice included Judah in what he had to say. The historic background reveals terrible decadence in Israel and Judah.

In view of this, the prophet was warning the nations of discipline in judgment, and the judgments predicted are progressive. Under figures of speech he describes two of them, and in definiteness of language the last. The first is found in verse twelve, " I am unto Ephraim as a moth " ; the second in verse fourteen, " I will be unto Ephraim as a lion " ; the last in verse fifteen, " I will go and return to My place."

The first judgment is described as that of the moth, that little insignificant insect, the moth, which nevertheless finds its way into the wealth of the East and destroys it. The second is referred to as that of the lion, rampant, angry, tearing, rending. And then the last, the most terrific of all, God withdrawing Himself, " I will go and return to My place, till . . . ! "

The warning is a solemn one. There can be none more solemn. The moth is a terrible thing. The lion is a terrible thing. But when God withdraws Himself, it is the most terrible calamity that can take place.

Nevertheless, it is at once to be noticed that this solemn warning ends on a note which reveals the Divine heart and intention. The first part of the

warning fills the heart with terror, " I will go and
return to My place " ; then comes the little word, the
arresting word, " till," and in that little word " till "
I discover the Divine heart. As we read it, and that
which follows, we discover the Divine intention, " I
will go and return to My place," but that is not My
will, or My desire, or what I want ; " till." Till what ?
" Till they acknowledge their offence, and seek My
face." Then the Divine word sings the song not
merely of hope, but of assurance, " In their affliction
they will seek Me earnestly."

Thus we have the most solemn warning, and coupled
with it a revelation of a method in the going, and a
final word which unveils the heart of God. To those
two matters, then, and in that sequence, let us give
our attention. Let us consider the solemnity of this
warning, the terrible calamity threatened; and then
the method in which the warning was given, as it
reveals the heart of God.

It is a strange word this, and a word that gives us
pause, that God said to these people that He would
leave them, that He would go, that He would withdraw
Himself, that He would return unto His place.

Of course the language is, to use theological terminology, the language of anthropomorphism, God speaking under the figure of Himself as a man as departing
and returning to His place. The meaning is perfectly
simple in one way. It means that He Who has been
present with them will withdraw from them. He
declares that under the conditions obtaining He will
go away.

In considering this warning, however, the limitation
of the idea must of necessity be observed. There is a

sense in which He is always present, whatever the wickedness, and whatever the rebellion. There is a sense in which His presence is never—and reverently let me say it—cannot be withdrawn. In the very nature of His Being that is so ; the actual presence is inescapable, the government of God is always active. His withdrawal does not mean that He is giving up His government. We must be very careful to understand these things. A startling illustration of the fact occurs in the later history, in the account of the night of carousal in the kingly halls of Belshazzar. We are all familiar with that story, dramatic and forceful, and flashing with revealing light. When Belshazzar, with a thousand of his lords, were drunk, when they had desecrated the vessels of the temple— which had been taken by them, and until then kept with a certain amount of sanctity—filling them with wine, and drinking from those very vessels until they were drunk, and their breath was consequently foul with drink and obscenity, there came the writing on the wall. " Mene, Mene, Tekel, Upharsin." In Daniel's interpretation of that writing, these startling words were spoken to the king, " The God in Whose hand thy breath is, and Whose are all thy ways, hast thou not glorified." In a sense God had withdrawn Himself, and calamity was coming. In another sense He had not withdrawn Himself. " Thy breath," the breath of Belshazzar, foul with drink and obscenity, " the God in Whose hand thy breath is." There is a sense in which God is never distanced, nor can be. There is a sense in which His government never ceases, for even when He says, " I will withdraw Myself," He is still acting in government.

This is a truth which lies at the heart of all life, which we should never forget. No man can escape the government of God. No man does escape from the government of God. We speak about men being rebels, and rebellious they are, in revolt against high heaven, lifting the blasphemous fist of wickedness, and smiting God in the face with intent ; but they never escape from His government. It is possible for me, in the mystery of my personality, to fling myself against the bosses on the shield of God ; but if I do, He breaks me ; He governs. It is possible for me to hide in penitence in the heart of God, and if I do, He heals me. But whether in law, or in grace, He governs. So also there are senses in which God is never withdrawn, for in Him we live and move and have our being. In His hand is our breath.

Then what does this mean ? It is self-evident that it means He would withdraw Himself in guidance. He would leave them to follow their own bent, abandon them to their own elections, their own choices, and their own decisions ; abandon them to the issue of those rebellions ; withdraw Himself from interference, from those activities of His Grace, which, in spite of their sin, had so long stood to prevent the ultimate calamity and loss. He said, " I will go and return to My place " ; and so allow you to go all the way that you are travelling ; I will raise no fresh barrier against you ; " I will go and return to My place."

Such withdrawal is the ultimate and direst calamity that can ever overtake a nation, any nation ; a man, any man ; for if God withdraw His interference, what have we lost ? We have lost the principle of holiness, the certainty of absolute wisdom, sufficient strength for the accomplishment of anything worth while, and the bringing of it to finality, and we have lost love.

If God withdraw Himself we may still attempt to set up standards of conduct by the consideration of circumstances, and they will break down ; for unless the spirit of holiness breathe through our ethical standards, they perish. Illustrations of this abound in human history. They are patent in the world to-day. When God withdraws Himself, then man has lost the true interpretation of holiness, and the only inspiration of holiness, and so the demand for holiness ceases. When God is withdrawn, men begin to declare that there is no such thing as holiness. But, it may be objected, we have not heard men say that. But we have heard them say there is no such thing as sin; and if there is no such thing as sin, there is no such thing as holiness. When God is withdrawn, the very distinction between right and wrong has gone. Morality is rooted in religion. When once religion —using the word in its high and proper sense, as the binding of man to God, and the holding of man in right relationship with God—whenever religion has perished, morality withers and dies, becomes the sport of the comic papers, the butt of brilliant articles in magazines, the ridicule of the philosophers who are without God. Holiness is at a discount. " I will withdraw Myself." When God does that, the vision and the passion for holiness perish.

Again, wisdom is lost. That is almost unbelievable. The age boasts itself in its knowledge. There is much wisdom which takes no account of God ; but is it wisdom ? Is knowledge ever wisdom when it shuts out of its calculation, at any point in human life, and

in any consideration, the supreme factor ? Can any
activity of the human mind lead man towards the
goal of human well-being, if God is eliminated ? All
such activity is of the essence of foolishness, nay more,
it is madness of the most destructive type.

If God withdraws Himself, it is equally true that
strength is withdrawn. There is a certain vitality of
flesh and of mind, for a while ; but if the spiritual
centre of life is dead, both the mental and the physical
wither, or become atrophied in all their highest
possibilities. Man cannot live by bread alone.

Finally, and most disastrously, if God withdraws
Himself, love will perish. John was right when he
said, " Love is of God." Much that is called love is
self-centred, and so lacks the vital principle which is
central to the love of God, and was the reason of that
self-emptying which brought Him to Calvary for us.

If that is the nature of this judgment, consider it
in its action. In the light of this prophecy, and in
the light of all the Biblical revelation, and in the light
of all human history, we are taught that God never
leaves man until man has left Him. Or—and I am
going to use very human language, because I know
none other — God never leaves man until He has
exhausted every method of discipline. First the moth,
then the lion, and only when those fail, withdrawal of
Himself. The moth, subtle, lacking in terror but
weakening in strength and resulting in decay of virility.
This is the act of God, intended to provoke man, in
the consciousness of weakness, to a rediscovery of,
and return to, the sources of strength. " I am unto
Ephraim as a moth, and to the house of Judah as
rottenness." The disaster was that Ephraim did

become conscious of his weakness, but did not return to God ; " When Ephraim saw his sickness, and Judah saw his wound, then went Ephraim to Assyria." The failure was with them. The purpose of the discipline of the moth was that of making the nation know its weakness that they might seek the sources of its strength, and it produced that effect—but they went to Assyria. Therefore the method of the moth was not enough.

Then, said God, I will take another method. I will become as a lion, and as a young lion to the house of Judah, " I, even I, will tear and go away ; I will carry off, and there shall be none to deliver." The judgment of swift and sudden and terrific calamity followed. What for ? Still, in order that the nation might be brought back to Him. Then, if this too fails, when every method of discipline intended to restore is exhausted, then the final and the terrific one is inevitable. God will withdraw ; " I will return to My place." God leaves man only when there is no hope in the case, nothing to which He can appeal, no avenue of approach, when every point of contact is destroyed.

No man can accurately interpret his own age. Distance alone gives true perspective. Nevertheless, it is impossible to read these pages without seeing light, flashing here and there, upon present conditions. To look back over half a century is to find at least reasons for solemn consideration. Necessarily my thoughts are concerned with my own country, but I think they have application to America also. Looking back now through the vista of these years, I am conscious of the method of the moth, the evidences of weakening in national character. And I do not see

that there was a return to God. Then came those
terrific years of the lion, and the young lion, of appalling
calamity, and catastrophe. And then I wonder, and
am uttering no final finding. Have these things
brought us back to God ? I am not answering the
question, but if not, then we stand, nationally, in
danger of this judgment of God ; that He may leave
us to our own courses.

Our very love of our nations, and our devotion to
their highest welfare, must make us almost poignantly
conscious of our peril, and must constrain us to prayer
that this thing may not happen, that God may not
withdraw Himself.

But do not forget this. He never does leave man
until man has left Him. " God was in Christ, recon-
ciling the world unto Himself." He had never left
the world. The world had left Him. There may be
inexactitudes of terminology in our best hymns. We
sing sometimes :

> " My God is reconciled,
>   His pardoning voice I hear.
> He owns me for His child,
>   I can no longer fear.
> With confidence I now draw nigh
> And Father, Abba, Father, cry."

I love that hymn. I shall undoubtedly sing it to the
end of the pilgrimage, and perhaps beyond—but
whenever I sing it, I think it a little differently in its
first line : " My God is reconciled." The deeper truth
is that I am reconciled to Him. He never turned His
back upon man, save as man turned his back upon
Him. He never gives man up, until something has
taken place in the individual soul, or in the condition

of the age, or in the national life, that has destroyed the possibility of contact. Said Jehovah, " I will go and return to My place." Why ? Because Israel and Judah had left Him, in spite of every attempt to hold them. God never leaves man until man leaves Him. He employs various methods of discipline ; every one of them intended to save us from our calamity, and bring us back, and hold us. But if there comes a moment when there is no response, then it is inevitable, not of His choice, but of our own selection, that He leave us.

But that is not all the text. I think if it were, I hardly dare talk about it. But it is not all. Even in that solemn and dread hour when, to Israel and Judah by the prophets Hosea and Isaiah, the case seemed so hopeless, that God withdrew Himself, He did so still with a note of hope. In all the other prophets we find the same principle. In Ezekiel, we find God withdrawing Himself from the temple and the people, but return and restoration are in view. When I read, " I will go and return to My place, till," like a flash that little word, equally simple in the language of which this is a translation, arrests thought in the presence of the terror, and the fact, using simple human language, that as God departs, He departs reluctantly, as though He said, I am going, but I do not want to go ; I am going to My place, because you will have none of Me ; but the door is open.

What infinite suggestions of compassion are in that little word " till " ! I find it again in equally arresting setting in the New Testament. Let me read the words again. They are found in Matthew xxiii. 37–39 :

" O Jerusalem, Jerusalem, that killeth the
prophets, and stoneth them that are sent unto
her ! how often would I have gathered thy
children together, even as a hen gathereth her
chickens under her wings, and ye would not !
Behold, your house is left unto you desolate.
For I say unto you, Ye shall not see Me henceforth, *till* ye shall say, Blessed is He that cometh
in the name of the Lord."

God on the page of the Old Testament, God on the
page of the New, abandoning a nation, abandoning a
city, abandoning a people, why ?   Because they would
not have Him.   I would have gathered your children
as a hen gathers her brood beneath her wings—
infinite and exquisite language, revealing the Motherhood of God—but ye would not ; therefore " your
house is left unto you desolate " ; and there is a fine
and caustic irony in it—*your* house, the temple.   He
had previously described it as " My Father's house,"
but at last He called it " your house," no longer God's
house.   As in the days of Hosea, Bethel, the House of
God, had become Bethaven, the house of vanity.
" Your house is left unto you desolate."

Is that all ?   Is doom the last word on the lips of
Jesus ?   No !   " Ye shall not see Me henceforth, till."
The door is open.   Oh, the gracious music, the infinite
harmonies of that one little word " *till*."   The warning
ends on a note, revealing His willingness to return.

To return to Hosea.   He tells them how He will
come back.   When will God come back ?   He said I
will leave you, till.   When will He return ?   Will He
indeed come back again, the God continually refused,

broken-hearted by the infidelity of His people ? He is bound to leave them, by the necessity of holiness and of love. When will He come back ? " Till they acknowledge their offence, and seek My face." First, when " they acknowledge their offence," that is, when they turn from their idols. And so, when they seek My face ; that is, when they return to God.

When Paul was writing his letter to the Thessalonians he described the whole of the Christian life by saying, " Ye turned to God from idols, to serve the living and true God, and to wait for His Son from heaven." From idols to God ; from sin to God ; from the folly of the long rebellion, back to God. That is all. When man turns back to God, God turns back to man.

Thus the solemn warning ends on the note of hope, of the door that is not shut. I will go to My place ; as though He said, But the door is open, it is on the latch. You can find Me if you want Me.

There is a story which comes back to me across the years. I tell it without any hesitation, because it illustrates this. It is the story of a mother in Scotland, and of her lassie who went wrong, broke with her home, went to the city, went down into the uttermost degradation. Mother did not know where she was, had not heard from her for ten long years. One night, broken and ruined and wrecked, Janet took her way home, and arrived there in the dead of night. She went up the little lane that led to the cottage, and when she got near, she saw a light burning in the window, and she was frightened, wondering whether her mother had gone, or was ill. What meant the light in the dead of night ? Softly she crept up till she got to the cottage itself, and put her hand on the latch, and she found the latch was open, the door was not locked ; and as she opened it, a voice said, " Is that you, Janet ? " Mother upstairs waiting for ten long years. Said the girl, " What is the light burning for, Mother ? I was afraid you were ill." " It has never been put out a night since you left, lassie, and the door has never been locked ! "

As a hen doth gather her chickens beneath her wings ! Till you acknowledge your offence and seek My face. When you do it, says God, the door is open. His judgments are terrible. They must be ; but the moth and the lion are intended to save us. And if we will not learn by the discipline, by the insidious weakening of all our forces ; and if we will not learn by the blood and muck and misery of war ; it may be God will have to say, I will go to My place, and leave you, leave you to your own devices, leave you *till* the point of contact is created anew. That point of contact can be made so far as God is concerned when we say, We will confess our sin, put away our idols, and come back seeking the face of God. The judgment is inevitable, made necessary by the choices of man when he turns from God ; but God leaves the door on the latch, and the light in the window !

In our preparatory reading for this meditation I included the first three verses of chapter six. I did so because they contain the prophet's appeal to the people to return to and through that door left open. It is one of the most tender and beautiful appeals to be found in the Bible. In our next study we will return to it for fuller consideration. In this we close by reading it :

> " Come, and let us return unto Jehovah ; for He hath torn, and He will heal us ; He hath smitten, and He will bind us up. After two days will He revive us : on the third day He will raise us up, and we shall live before Him. And let us know, let us follow on to know Jehovah : His going forth is sure as the morning ; and He will come unto us as the rain, as the latter rain that watereth the earth."

V

THE DIFFICULTY OF GOD

HOSEA vi. 4–11

" O Ephraim, what shall I do unto thee ? O Judah,
what shall I do unto thee ? for your goodness is as a
morning cloud, and as the dew that goeth early away."
—HOSEA vi. 4.

As we take our way through this prophecy we find in
it a wonderful revelation of the struggle of God over
the soul of a nation.   Its messages alternate between
the passion of the Divine heart and the perversity of
the human will.

We were concerned in our previous meditation with
the final verse of the previous chapter. " I will go
and return to My place, till they acknowledge their
offence, and seek My face."   That is the ultimate
judgment of God upon a sinning people, the withdrawal of Himself, the withdrawal of His presence,
that is in the sense of guiding or governing ;   the
abandonment of the people to their own elections,
and their own choices, and their own perversities.
But we saw that the solemn word of warning ended
with the leaving open of the door.   He said, " I will
go and return to My place, till " ; and the way of
return was indicated, " Till they acknowledge their
offence, and seek My face " ; God was revealed as not
willing to abandon, even when He withdrew Himself.

The chapter from which the text is taken is linked
with the preceding one, in the sequence of teaching,
for directly the prophet had uttered that solemn word
that told of the Divine withdrawal, and ended with the
note that indicated the door was still open for the
return of His people if they would acknowledge their
offence and seek His face, he broke out into what is
certainly one of the most tender and beautiful appeals
of all the Biblical literature, contained in the first
three verses of chapter six, and to which we will
return presently.   The prophet said to the people, in
view of the illuminative word of imminent judgment, and of the fact that in uttering it God had
indicated His willingness to return, " Come, and let
us return unto Jehovah ; for He hath torn, and He
will heal us." It was a great appeal, thrilling with
Messianic promise, the final meaning of which was
never found until in the fulness of time the Messiah
came, while yet it had an immediate value for those
who heard it.

Then suddenly, breaking in upon that plaintive and
beautiful appeal, the voice of God is heard :   " O
Ephraim, what shall I do unto thee ?   O Judah, what
shall I do unto *thee* ? for your goodness is as a morning
cloud, and as the dew that goeth early away."   It is
a strange and startling word, declaring the difficulty
of God ; " What shall I do ? . . . what shall I do ? "
It also reveals the reason for the difficulty :   " Your
goodness is as a morning cloud, and as the dew that
goeth early away."

Let us consider first the fact as disclosed, the
difficulty of God ; and that in order that we may
inquire, Is there any solution ?   God is seen in

difficulty. Is there any way of escape for God from His difficulty ?

God's difficulty is revealed, as I have said, in the question He asks. It is a daring figure of speech which the prophet employed, and of course that means that God employed it through His servant the prophet. I think the more quietly we look at it, and the more carefully we consider it, the more startling it will become. I can understand a man saying, What shall I do to be saved ? But here is God saying, What shall I do to save him ? This is not the cry of the human soul seeking after God. It is the cry of God seeking after the human soul. This is not the picture of a man in difficulty because he cannot find God. It is the picture of God in difficulty because He cannot deal with man. " O Ephraim, what shall I do unto thee ? O Judah, what shall I do unto thee ? "

The same attitude is revealed more than once in the course of these prophetic writings in the Old Testament. The great song of the vineyard in the beginning of chapter five in the prophecy of Isaiah opens ; " Let Me sing for My well-beloved a song of My beloved touching His vineyard. My well-beloved had a vineyard in a very fruitful hill . . . and he looked that it should bring forth grapes, and it brought forth wild grapes." Then interpreting the parable, God is recorded as saying, " What could have been done more to My vineyard, that I have not done in it ? " Said Hosea in the northern kingdom, " O Ephraim, what shall I do unto thee ? O Judah, what shall I do unto thee ? " and in the southern kingdom, contemporary with Hosea, Isaiah was saying the same thing. He was declaring that God was faced with

difficulty; " What could have been done more to
My vineyard, that I have not done ? " And yet
another prophet, also exercising his ministry in the
same period, Micah, makes God thus speak : " O My
people, what have I done unto thee ? and wherein
have I wearied thee ? Testify against Me." In all
those messages the attitude of God revealed is very
arresting.

Now bluntly, what does this mean ? Wherein lies
the Divine difficulty ? Why this appeal of God in
extremity, and in difficulty, in the presence of a
nation, or of a human soul ? What does it mean ?
The answer to that question is clearly given. The
reason He gives for His difficulty is not their sin, is
not that of their pollution. It is true that the whole
prophecy pulsates with the unveiling of their lewdness
and whoredom and drunkenness and beastliness ; but
these are not the things that constitute the difficulty
of God. When He speaks of His difficulty He does
not say a word about their sin.

What, then, constitutes His difficulty ? Their
goodness. That is the trouble. " For your goodness
is as a morning cloud, and the dew which goeth early
away." Now here we surely discover an element
that startles us ; God in difficulty in the presence of
goodness !

Mark well the figures of speech. A morning cloud,
and dew. They are both things of excellence, and
things of exquisite beauty. The morning cloud, as
the sun is rising, is smitten with beauty ; and dew in
the beauty of the morning, when every blade of grass
is glistening in rainbow loveliness, is equally glorious.
The morning cloud is a thing of exquisite beauty, and

the dew a thing of infinite tenderness. " O Ephraim, what shall I do unto you ? O Judah, what shall I do unto thee ? for your goodness is as a morning cloud and as the dew."

But read on, and we have the revealing expression, " which goeth early away." A morning cloud, the dew ; both excellent, but evanescent ; too feeble to produce a harvest, dissipated by the heat of the sun, ere any permanent result can be gained. Goodness evanescent, that is what creates God's difficulty. I am quite willing to put this superlatively. God's difficulty is not created by vulgar sins ; God's difficulty is not created in the human soul by reason of pollution and whoredom and beastliness. With these things God can deal ; but God is in great difficulty when goodness is only like the morning cloud, is only like the dew that goeth early away.

What is goodness ? In the margin of the King James Version you will notice that it is suggested that instead of the word " goodness " we should read " mercy or kindness " ; and the Revisers, English and American, suggest " kindness." " Your kindness is as a morning cloud, and as the dew that goeth early away." But we must examine that a little more closely. The Hebrew word rendered goodness has as its root meaning, the idea of bending the neck ; and in use it was constantly employed as referring to the attitude of graciousness, and of goodness in that sense. Here I think that neither word, goodness nor kindness, catches the real idea of the complaint of God. The word suggests that attitude of life which bends the neck, and I would, while recognizing that the word connotes goodness, and is a revelation of

the very essence of kindness, render it thus : " O
Ephraim, what shall I do unto thee ? O Judah, what
shall I do unto thee ? for your *submission* is as a
morning cloud." Goodness is right, because all goodness is the result of submission to God ; and kindness
is right, because all kindness issues from such submission ; but here it is important to get back to the
first meaning of the word. It is a revelation of what
goodness really is, and so a revelation of the difficulty
of God. I am reverently attempting to interpret
from the Divine standpoint. God had said, I will
withdraw Myself, and go to My place, and leave these
people to their own choices and devices and imaginings,
till they seek My face. Then God, through the
prophet, called them to return. And, suddenly, God
said ; Yes, but that is indeed the trouble. In their
returning there has been no resoluteness, no abiding
value. They have come back so often, but their
coming has meant nothing. They have bent the neck
sincerely, but all their submission has been evanescent.

Now that is the point when God is in difficulty with
men. My sins, my sins like mountains rise, but He
can deal with them ; but my goodness, my submission
which ends with admiration, aspiration, intention,
and then passes, creates the difficulty of God.

Do not let us misunderstand this. These things are
valuable. They are worth-while things. The attitude,
whether we render it kindness or goodness, is rooted
in submission, and that is wholly excellent. Submission always begins with admiration of the ideal,
and proceeds along the line of aspiration unto realization. It is in essence, intention to fulfil aspiration,
and realize the ideal.

How often men come there quite sincerely. There was no hypocrisy in that high moment, when seeing the vision of the ideal as revealed in ideal relationship with God, we admired, we aspired, we intended. But if there was no ultimate realization, it was all worthless. The experience of such an hour may abide with us as something to be trusted in, when the life is not squaring with the experience of the hour. Very many people are living there. There was a moment away in the past, when we admired, when we aspired, when we intended, when we devoted ourselves. Are we living content with the fact that we had such an hour? There is no value in that. Unless the admiration, and aspiration, and intention have produced abiding result, a harvest of fruitfulness, of realization, there is no value in such an experience. So far from being of value, it reacts upon the conscience and deadens it. When men trust in the morning cloud, and the dew that once appeared, God says, What can I do? How am I to reach you behind that? " O Ephraim, what shall I do unto thee? O Judah, what shall I do unto thee?"

Let us press that matter home, and ask ourselves why is it that men ever fail in this way? How is it that we have so often had that kind of experience?

Goodness as here described, and the whole attitude of the life referred to, moves in the realm of feeling. Evanescent goodness, evanescent submission to God, is always the result of superficial feeling. Some one will ask, Is feeling wrong? I reply, not only is it not wrong, it is absolutely necessary. But it is not the ultimate thing; and unless feeling be answered by certain attitudes and activities of personality, it is always evanescent. Feeling has its place. Feeling has its value. Feeling is absolutely necessary. But it is not enough in itself.

Henry Ward Beecher once said : " Feeling is to action what wind is to the sails of a vessel." That is an arresting and illuminative saying. If there is too little wind, there is no progress. If there is too much wind, there is wreckage. If the vessel is to be propelled, there must be a sufficient amount of wind. If the wind become a tornado the vessel is in danger of becoming a wreck. The illustration teaches us that feeling must be in control and reinforced in some way, or else it becomes evanescent. The trouble with many too often is that feeling is not deep enough, and that is why goodness is evanescent. Sometimes, on the other hand, feeling is too much, emotion sweeps a man off his feet, and makes him lose his mental poise. When it does, it destroys the religious instinct and power.

Now let us remember that feeling always results from the appeal of intellect. I do not need to discuss that metaphysically or psychologically. The fact is self-evident. We never felt anything but as the result of the combination of the emotion with the intellect. Feeling always results from the appeal to the intellect. Goodness came ; I saw the ideal ; I admired it, I aspired after it ; I intended to realize it. Feeling was there, but it was response to revelation, revelation of the beauty of the ideal, revelation of the glory of the ideal.

Why, then, was it evanescent ? Feeling is evanescent when it fails to strike downwards to the facts producing it ; and facing those facts, to arrange the life in harmony therewith. A superficial grasp upon the truth concerning God will produce feelings, approbation, admiration, aspiration, intention ; but unless we then turn round, and facing these facts, seeing their bearing upon life, act accordingly, goodness will be as evanescent as the morning cloud, and as the early dew.

Goodness, as submission, is response to conviction about God. There is the trouble oftentimes. We do not face the facts until our whole life is rooted in them, and so fail to reach the realm of permanence in our goodness. We often recite the Apostles' Creed, and we mean what we say, but fail to act accordingly. Its great opening affirmation is a fundamental revelation : " I believe in God." We say it, and in the saying are sincere. In the saying of it we are telling the truth. In the saying of it we are giving expression to an intellectual concept and conviction. Moreover, in the saying of it, in the very fact that we do say it, whether we say it alone or in an assembly, there is proof of an emotional activity resulting from an intellectual conviction. We do believe in God, and in the very affirmation of the fact there is a glow and a glory. Then—what then ? Having said it we leave the sanctuary, and pass back to the everyday life and the workaday days, and the busy world. Have we faced seriously the thing we affirmed as our creed ? Have we considered the implicates of our declaration ? Are we now arranging our life in accord with our creed ? If not, then our goodness is as the morning cloud, very real, very excellent, touched with rainbow hues of beauty and colour and heavenly glory, but quite useless unless we strike downwards to the intellectual concept that produced the goodness of the moment. If we fail there, the goodness, the emotional submission will all evaporate, it will bring forth no results in life. That is God's difficulty. And that is why it is more difficult to preach the Gospel to a respectable congregation than in a Rescue Mission. The trouble is not with the iniquities of such a congregation, but with its shallowness. Thomas Champness once said, " If God made the country, and man made the city ; the devil made the suburbs." From the religious standpoint, there is an element of truth in the statement. God has greater difficulty in dealing with people who know goodness and admire goodness, but whose goodness is evanescent, the goodness of a cloud in the morning, flecked with sunlight ; or dew, all to be burnt up and dissipated in the heats of the day, than He has with the man we call down-and-out. " O Ephraim, what shall I do ? Judah, what shall I do ? "

But another reason why goodness is evanescent is that feeling admits other motives, fails to concentrate, admits other appeals before the one is settled. Mixed motives, the divided heart, these are destructive of goodness. The prayer of the Psalmist was, " O Lord, unite my heart to fear Thy name." " One thing I do," said Paul, " I press toward the mark." That did not mean for a single moment that Paul only did one thing as to the details of life. Think of what he did, the journeys he took, the letters he wrote, the many and varied interests that crowded upon his life. Yes, but all the duties were unified by the doing of one thing. That is too often the trouble with us. First we do not investigate the thing that produces the passing glow and glory of our submission ; and then we allow other motives to come in side by side with it. Those are the reasons why goodness is evanescent.

Now let us turn to our second inquiry. Is there any solution to this problem ? To put it in another way, is there any cure for this evanescent goodness ? There is. But it is in man, and not in God. Immediately after the question revealing the difficulties of God we find this statement, " I desire goodness and not sacrifice." We cannot atone for the evanescent nature of our goodness with our gifts. Let us read on : " I desire the knowledge of God more than burnt offerings."

Well then, what is God to do ? That is not the question. " What shall I do ? " " I desire goodness," " I desire the knowledge of God." God might have said, as indeed He did say, I have made known Myself to you by the prophets, but you will not answer the revelation. I repeat, the solution must be found in man.

But that is not the final word. To find it we must go back to the appeal at the beginning of the chapter :

> " Come, and let us return unto Jehovah ; for He hath torn, and He will heal us ; He hath smitten, and He will bind us up. After two days will He revive us ; on the third day He will raise us up, and we shall live before Him. And let us know, let us follow on to know Jehovah."

Underline the words " let us " in that paragraph. " Let us return, let us know, let us follow on to know." If we obey those injunctions, we solve God's difficulty and satisfy God's heart. " Let us return," and " let us know " ; and it is the next thing that is of supreme importance ; " let us follow on to know."

Then underline the words " He will." What do we find ? " He will heal," " He will bind up," " He will revive us," " He will raise us up," " He will come unto us as the rain, as the latter rain."

That is what He wants to do. That is what He is waiting to do. I have no language but the human, and there can be no interpretation of God ultimately but in human language. In these words we hear the sob of the heart of God after these people.

" What shall I do ? " What shall Jehovah do ? Blast them, damn them, sweep them out ? That is not God. And if ever man is blasted ultimately, damned finally, swept down into the darkling void where God is not, it will be by his own choice, and never by the will of the heart of God. " God willeth not the death of a sinner." In these words there is the threnody of an infinite compassion, " Ephraim, what shall I do ? Judah, what shall I do ? " My trouble with you is that your goodness is like a morning cloud, like the dew that vanishes. As though God said, I can deal with your lewdness ; I can deal with your beastliness, if you turn back to Me ; but I cannot deal with you while you are living in the realm of an evanescent goodness that never strikes its roots, and so produces fruit.

Where are we living ? No, do not ask where I am living, and I will not ask where you are living. You have no right to investigate for me, and I have no right to investigate for you. But let us investigate our own lives in the light of the revelation. I wonder if God is saying of any of us, The trouble with you is that your goodness is like a morning cloud, like the dew that vanishes early. Admiration, aspiration, good intention ; but evanescent ; and because the things admired are not investigated, and life is not readjusted in harmony with those things desired, there is failure.

Deepen the wounds Thy hands have made, O God of love, until goodness shall be to us the result of Thy coming, and Thy healing, Thy binding, Thy reviving ; the latter rain that produces the harvest. Shall we not deliver God from the difficulty that confronts His love by returning, and knowing, and following on to know.

VI

UNCONSCIOUS DECADENCE

HOSEA vii.

"Gray hairs are here and there upon him, and he knoweth it not."—HOSEA vii. 9*b*.

Or, to read that in slightly different form, a more literal rendering of the Hebrew, and I think perhaps a more poetic : "Gray hairs are sprinkled upon him, and he knoweth it not."

THIS is without question a terrible chapter. It is a prophetic diagnosis of the national condition. The dark and terribly sinister background of a degenerate and polluted people is of course patent throughout the book. In this message, however, the prophet deals with it very definitely. He shows that the desire of God is to heal and to restore ; but that this desire is constantly frustrated by the pollution of the nation, and its wilful ignoring of God. In difficulty politically, and with regard to surrounding peoples, it is running to Assyria and to Egypt for help. I repeat, there is persistent ignoring of God, and all the while its strength is ebbing away. The nation is being destroyed.

The verse from which the text is taken repeats the same phrase twice over, "knoweth it not." The statement is first made, "Strangers have devoured his strength, and he *knoweth it not*"; and then is repeated pictorially, " Yea, gray hairs are sprinkled upon him, and he knoweth it not." The tragedy of the situation is revealed in that twice-repeated word, " he knoweth it not . . . he knoweth it not." " Gray hairs are here and there upon him, and he knoweth it not." It is perhaps the most perilous condition possible.

The first thing I would like to say in considering the figure employed is that the suggestion it makes is entirely contrary to Nature. Now I ask you, if any of you were unconscious when the gray hairs began to appear ! I do not think any one would claim such ignorance. It is never so in actual experience. We discover the gray hairs, some of us sooner than others, but we discover them ! So here is something employed as a figure of speech which is contrary to Nature, and therefore is the more arresting. Men discover them, and they laugh at them, or they try to hide them, or if they are foolishly weak-minded, they pull them out, and if they are utterly stupid they dye them. I said *men* ! The facts as stated may have wider application. I am content to refer to men only !

" Gray hairs are here and there upon him, and he knoweth it not." It is not natural, it is not true. If it were ever true in the time of the prophet then mirrors were not plentiful. Mirrors are useful if only that they do help us to discover the gray hairs. And yet the prophet distinctly said of the nation : " Gray hairs are here and there upon him, and he knoweth it not."

And yet, this thing entirely unnatural in the physical, is constantly true in the moral and spiritual realms, and so the figure of the prophet is warranted and indeed most graphic. Signs of decadence, which are patent to others, are undiscovered by ourselves ; and we go on, and on, and on, the victims of ebbing strength, spiritually and morally becoming degenerate, without knowing it ! We are blind to the signs which are self-evident to onlookers. There is no condition more perilous to our highest well-being than this of unconscious decadence. The skilful physician knows how often the cessation of suffering means that mortification has set in, and that in the moral realm may be the meaning of ignorance of gray hairs.

There is one text in the Bible that, as God is my witness, I never read without trembling. It is a text that tells the story of Samson : " He wist not that the Spirit of God had departed from him." A man who had known the power of the Holy Spirit resting upon him, working through him, was going on and on, and the Spirit had left him, and he did not know it. " Gray hairs are here and there upon him, and he knoweth it not." The signs of moral and spiritual degeneracy are abounding, and they are seen by others, but not by ourselves. I repeat, there is no condition into which a man or a nation can pass more full of peril, more calamitous than that. Moral degeneracy and spiritual failure are cursing them, and all the while they are unconscious of it, going through the same motions, but without vital significance. It may be, to be particular and immediate, they are still going to church every Sunday, saying their prayers every night, making their contribution to the enterprises of God in the world with regularity, and yet all the while suffering from spiritual degeneracy and moral pollution.

The change is apparent to others, the signs of weakness are patent, but they do not know it.

In considering this matter, let us follow three lines of inquiry : What is the cause of this ignorance ? What its course ? And what its cure ?

First, then, what is the cause of such ignorance ? I am not now talking about the disease. I am talking rather and only about the appalling condition of having the disease and not knowing it, of having moral and spiritual declension and being unconscious of it. Why is it that men are ever thus unconscious of that which is patent to others ?

The first answer to this is that a man who is unconscious of his own moral degeneracy and spiritual deflection is a man who has lost his vision of the normal. When I use the word " normal " I am using the word on its highest level. I am thinking for the moment not socially, or nationally, but individually. I am thinking of individual lives, according to the Divine standard and pattern, according to the ideal. Here, moreover, I am not concerned with ideals we have created for ourselves, but with the ideals which lie potentially within our personalities, the ideals— let it be said bluntly, the ideals of God for us.

If a man is unconscious of failure, it is because he has lost a sense of true standards ; the reason is always that he has lost his vision of the true norm, even though he may still talk about the ideal. When he speaks of the ideal, what he means is not the ideal. The trouble with men and women everywhere who have gray hairs upon them in the moral and spiritual realm, and do not know it, is that they have lost the true vision of the norm.

The normal in man, what is it ?   First of all, his
spiritual nature ;   secondly, the fact that holiness is
for evermore the condition of beauty and health ;   and,
therefore, that the mental and the physical in human
personality are subservient to the spiritual, and only
valuable as they are sacramental symbols of that
spiritual essence.   It will be admitted that men to-day
are not so thinking of human life.   And that is the
trouble with man to-day, he is thinking about himself
meanly.   Or to return to the statement already made,
men have lost the vision of the normal.

How do we think about human life ?   How is it to
be interpreted ?   What is the ideal ?   We lose the
sense of the normal in human life when we forget that
the supreme fact of personality is neither physical nor
psychical, but pneumatic.   I do not quite like using
that word, because to-day we have lost its first value.
We use it about tyres !   Pneumatic in the Scriptural
sense means spiritual.   Moral degeneracy, why ?
Because man is forgetting the majesty and the dignity
of his personality, and that the ideal of man's life is
never accurate when the spiritual is either neglected
or a contradicted quantity in his life.   A man may
be quite moral according to the standards of life
to-day, and yet in the deepest sense be immoral.   We
say a man is a decent member of society ?   But what
do we mean by society ?   Ordinary society, everyday
society, intellectual society, æsthetic society, refined
society ?   I am not denying that a man may be decent
in those surroundings.   But how does he feel when
he gets into a prayer meeting ?   Oh, he says—" I
don't go."   We know that.   But why doesn't he go ?
Because he feels he would be out of place there.

Exactly, he has lost the sense of the fact that man at his highest is a man who communes with God ; that the ultimate vocation of human life is not the functioning of the fussy days in which we are gathering ducats and dollars ; that the ultimate meaning of human life is fulfilled when a man walks and talks with God. If he have lost that, then gray hairs are upon him, and he doesn't know it, because that is not his vision.

This lost sense of the spiritual nature of man always issues in a lowered conviction concerning holiness, the forgetfulness of the fact that holiness is the condition of beauty ; and that there is no beauty in the ultimate meaning of the great and gracious word, except the beauty of holiness, that which results from holiness. It may be objected that this is a very old-fashioned conception of life, indeed Victorian or puritanical. As a matter of fact it is much older than that. It is as old as man is, and older ; it is as old as the foundation of the universe, as old as the philosophy that realizes that all things proceed from God. It is lost irrevocably by men who have lost contact with God. When we have lost a sense of the spiritual, and the deep inner conviction that the secret of all beauty is holiness, and that the mental and the physical, sacred things, Divinely created things, are, after all, in the last analysis, subservient to the spiritual, we have lost our sense of the normal in human life.

The vision of the normal declares that the cardinal things of beauty and of splendour in human life are faith and hope and love. Faith, which is the substance of things hoped for, and the evidence of things not seen ; faith, that faculty of the human soul that always soars from the rock of reason, but presently spreads its pinions and reaches the Infinite, and has fellowship with it. Faith, which grasps the Eternal in its thinking, and then compels conduct to conform to the vision. Faith is never dead. It is always the principle of energy. Nothing was ever done, of human worth, but was done on the basis of faith. Every victory ever won individually or socially resulted from the activity of faith. Every deed is preceded by a dream. When we were young they told us, sometimes, alas, cynically, we were building castles in the air. Of course we were. Normal human life always begins there. Have you a boy doing it at home? Don't you dare be fool enough to sneer at your boy for building his castle in the air. That is faith. No boy ever built a cottage on the ground but that it had been preceded by a castle in the air. That is faith. It was faith which spanned the rivers and tunnelled the mountains; faith did the engineering feats that fill us with wonder as we travel, winding round and round the mountains, or boring through their fast-nesses. When faith only operates within the limits of the material, and does not go out into the realm where no bridges can be built and no tunnels made, there is an atrophy of personality. Then we have lost our vision of the normal. Where faith is for evermore interpreting and making real the things not yet grasped and not yet reached, for evermore building castles, not in the air, but in the vastness of eternity, and in the ages to come, then life is normal. No achievement within the physical is final or complete. No city of human construction is perfect. The ultimate city must come down out of heaven from God. For the building of that, faith is supremely necessary.

God grant that we may be enabled to see again the norm of human life, the real meaning of being, to catch again the consciousness of the norm in grandeur and splendour, with the spiritual central to everything ; holiness the condition of beauty ; mental and physical powers subject to spiritual aspirations and endeavours. That is faith grasping the infinite, hope aspiring toward realization, and love harmonizing with the pulsing heart of God. If we do not see that vision, then let us look in a mirror, and we shall see the gray hairs.

This loss of the vision of the normal issues in the setting up of false standards of life. Denying the spiritual there follows the apotheosis of the mental, and the deification of the physical. When these things are so, personality is degenerate ; it is working its own destruction.

Of course the trouble too often is that men are satisfied with comparing themselves with the average man, a terrible thing to do. The average man is the man who does not know, does not see that the Spirit of God has departed. Too many to-day are like the group in Ephesus who said—as the King James Version renders it—" We have not so much as heard whether there be any Holy Ghost."

Of this condition of unconscious decadence we have another prophetic illustration in Malachi. Seven times over across the page of Malachi it is recorded that the people replied to the prophetic messages by asking the same question, " Wherein ? " Here we have the same people later on saying, " Wherein." The prophet said, You have robbed God ; and they replied in effect : We do not see we have robbed Him ;

wherein have we done so ? He charged them with
blasphemy. They said, Wherein have we blasphemed ?
That is what the world is saying to-day to the preacher :
What is all this about ? Wherein have we failed ?
What is the matter with us ? Why do you preach to
us ? Why do you do it ? Wherein are we wrong ?
I will tell you what is the matter. Gray hairs are
here and there upon men, and they do not know it.
Spiritual declension, moral deterioration, lowering of
the standards, a loosening of the high ideals of beauty
and holiness ; and men do not see it, do not know it,
because they have lost the vision of the true ideal,
and therefore they have set up false ideals. A debased
ideal issues in a degenerate personality ; but men are
unconscious of the destructive process.

Now a second line of consideration is involved, that
of the curse of this ignorance. Signs of decadence
witness to debility and disease ; and they are really
beneficent warnings if we did but see them. To return
to the realm of Nature. Gray hairs are a beneficent
warning. They are at least to remind us that we are
to limit our output of energy. Every indication of
degeneracy is a warning. It might be possible for a
man to grow old without any sign to warn him as to
how he should conduct his affairs. That would but
hasten the end of everything. The signs are beneficent
warnings, but when they are undiscovered, the warning
is not known, but the disease is still there, and its
operation is progressive, and its ultimate is death.

Are we conscious that between the to-day of our
experience and the yesterday of it, five, ten years ago,
there is a lowering of our moral standards ? If we
are not, our neighbours are, and our mothers are, our

wives are, and our husbands are, and our children are !
It is indeed a tragedy if we are blind to it when it is
there. The warning is unheeded because the sign is
not discovered ; but the trouble is there, and the
process is going on. Ephraim, not knowing that gray
hairs were here and there upon him nationally, was
degenerate, and the degeneracy was progressive, and
the ultimate must be destruction.

Gray hair is not a tragedy ; but failure to see it is.
An unconsciousness which produces carelessness is in
itself a catastrophe. Spiritual and moral failure is a
tragedy, accentuated a thousand-fold by ignorance of it.

Thus we come to our final inquiry. Is there any
cure for this ignorance ? The answer is involved in
the previous considerations. The cure for ignorance
is found in the contemplation of the normal. And
this is now made possible to us in a Person. How
much time do we give to see Jesus clearly for ourselves. I know, and I am not unconscious of the value
of it so far as it goes, that we have a general familiarity
with Him, that we even give our assent to the great
doctrines of the Church concerning Him. But how
much time do we give to personally consider Him ?
There is no correction more quick, and sharp, and
powerful to my own spiritual and moral carelessness
and blindness than determined consideration of the
Normal and the Ideal of my human nature, as it is
given to me in the Person of Christ. Consideration of
Him means the restoration of the vision of the Normal.
If we will honestly give ourselves to the business of
considering Him, such consideration will bring quick
and sharp revelation of the sprinkling of the gray
hairs, of the sense of failure in ourselves. It always

has been so, and always will be so to the end of the
journey.   To see the failure is at least to be a long
way towards recovery.   To know that the Spirit of
God has left me at least gives me the opportunity for
investigating the reason for His departure, and seeking
again to find Him.

Of course contemplation of the normal must be
followed by severe and honest self-examination by
that Norm.   How often do we examine ourselves ?
How often do we take time to see how far are we from
these ideals ?   Wherein are we coming short ?   Do
not expect any one else to do this for you.   They
cannot.   You could not for me, nor I for you.   We
cannot examine each other in the last analysis.   But
if we will ourselves bring our lives to the test of the
revelation that God has given us in the Man of Galilee,
and that not merely with regard to the outward conditions of life, but to the inward thinking of life, not
merely with regard to the things that are overt and
open before the eyes of others, but with regard to
those inner and spiritual centres of life, it will be a
severe and healthful discipline for us spiritually.

But again, the vision of the normal and of the actual,
by the way of severe self-examination, will reveal the
gray hairs, but it will not remove them.   If they are
there, even though I see the Normal, the sight of the
Normal will not remove them.   If they are there,
even though I am brought to a consciousness of failure,
that consciousness is not enough to overtake it and
correct it.

Then what shall we do ?   We must turn to God.
To return to those half humorous things we were
saying at the beginning.   The gray hairs which

pictorially set forth spiritual and moral weakness, degeneracy, deflection ; the gray hairs ; well, what about them ? God does not laugh at them, and God won't help us to hide them, so that they cannot be seen ; and God won't pull up symptoms and leave the disease, and God will have no fellowship in the lying work of dyeing them another colour. What will He do ?

As we are in the Old Testament we will first consult it for an answer. Listen to this :

> " Jehovah, Who forgiveth all thine iniquities ; Who healeth all thy diseases ; Who redeemeth thy life from destruction ; Who crowneth thee with loving-kindness and tender mercies; Who satisfieth thy desire with good things, so that thy youth is renewed like the eagle."

Then the gray hairs disappear. That is a psalm.

Let me turn over to a prophet preaching at the same time Hosea was, namely, Isaiah :

> " They that wait for Jehovah shall renew their strength. They shall mount up with wings as eagles ; they shall run and not be weary ; they shall walk and not faint."

God alone is able to remove gray hairs from our spiritual and moral nature by taking away the destructive forces of our strength which are producing the moral degeneracy.

Let us turn to the New Testament and finish there. What is the cure for gray hairs, moral and spiritual ? What is the cure for signs of disease ? What is the way by which the evidences of senility morally and spiritually can be banished for ever ?   What is the way ?

"Ye must be born again."

The new life that He gives will remove the disease, and put an end to the signs of weakness.   May God arouse us if we are asleep, open our eyes if blind, so that it may not be true of us that the gray hairs are there without our knowing it.

VII

GOD MISLAID

HOSEA viii.

"For Israel hath forgotten his Maker, and builded palaces ; and Judah hath multiplied fortified cities : but I will send a fire upon his cities, and it shall devour the castles thereof."—HOSEA viii. 14.

THAT is the final verse in a chapter which contains a message of judgment, judgment in the sense of punishment and calamity about to fall upon the people. The chapter is dramatic in its method. It opens with two clarion cries ; and our translators have just a little robbed the passage of its arresting character by the introduction of certain words, in order to euphony, and the making of smooth reading and sense. There is something of value in the very method of abruptness and arousal. In our Bibles the first verse reads :

"Set the trumpet to thy mouth. As an eagle he cometh against the house of Jehovah, because they have transgressed My covenant, and trespassed against My law."

The first word there is the word "set." There is no such word in the Hebrew text. It has been supplied. And again, in the sentence "as an eagle he cometh," the words "he cometh" do not occur in the Hebrew text. They have been supplied. Now, if we are seeking for beauty of literature merely, according to our English standards, all that may be very good ; but I am simply drawing attention to the fact that in the Hebrew text there is an abruptness about it. Two clarion cries sharply follow : the first, " The trumpet to thy mouth " ; the second, " As an eagle against the house of Jehovah." The text does not say " Set " ; it does not say " He cometh." As a matter of fact, we have not improved it from the literary standpoint by the introduction of these words. The method of the Hebrew suggests two sudden trumpet blasts. The message of the prophet was intended to be one of arousal ; and it began with those two clarion cries : " The trumpet to thy mouth," " As an eagle against the house of Jehovah."

Now I do not know anything experimentally about the playing of a trumpet, but I do know that the Hebrew word here means, The trumpet to the roof of your mouth. Is there some peculiar, wailing sound produced by that action ? I don't know ; but it is a startling word, " The trumpet to the roof of the mouth. As an eagle against the house of Jehovah." Then the prophet runs on, " Because they have trans-gressed My covenant, and trespassed against My law. They shall cry unto Me, My God, we Israel know Thee. Israel hath cast off that which is good ; the enemy shall pursue him "—and so forth.

The chapter, I repeat, is a chapter of judgment, and if it be carefully examined it will be found that the prophet gives the reasons for the calamity which he is declaring to be imminent ; and it is as though he does so in five blasts upon the trumpet. Or, in

other words, he names five causes of the coming judgments, and he does so with a crescendo effect as he
reveals the failure and the sin of the nation. What
are the five charges he makes against them ? First,
transgression and trespass ; secondly, false kings and
princes set up to rule without consulting God ; thirdly,
idolatry, the calf of Samaria set up as a centre of
worship ; fourthly, the folly of seeking safety in
alliance with Assyria ; fifthly, false altars, and sin as
the result of them. That is all the chapter, until we
reach our text.

Then in the words of the text he summarizes the
whole situation.

> " Israel hath forgotten his Maker, and builded
> palaces ; and Judah hath multiplied fortified
> cities ; I will send a fire upon his cities, and it
> shall devour the castles thereof."

This, then, is clearly a message of judgment, and in
these words we find the prophet's declaration of the
all-containing malady, of which all the other things are
symptoms.

What, then, is the malady ? That is inclusively
stated in the words, " Israel hath forgotten his Maker."
Having made this inclusive statement, the prophet
describes the resulting activity of the people who have
forgotten their Maker. In this charge Judah is
implicated as well as Israel. There are two activities
described. " Israel hath builded palaces," and " Judah
hath multiplied fortified cities." The activities which
result when the people have forgotten God, are—
building palaces, and multiplying fortified cities. The
final word is the declaration of judgment, " I will send

fire upon the cities . . . and destroy the castles."
Let us follow the lines suggested, considering : the
All-containing Malady ; the Resulting Activity ; the
Issue.

The all-containing malady. " Israel hath forgotten
his Maker." Every one knows what it is to forget.
But do we ? Does this mean that the nation of Israel
and of Judah—Hosea speaking specially to Israel,
but ever and anon, as we have seen, talking to Judah
as implicated in the wrongdoing of Israel, and so
including the whole nation—does this mean, I say, that
these people had really forgotten God in the usual
sense of the word ? By no means ! Men cannot
forget God. They can deny Him, but in so doing they
are still remembering Him ! Men do not forget God
intellectually. This nation certainly had not forgotten
God in that first and simple sense of the word. What
then is this idea of forgetting God ? In order to understand the statement, to see the real significance of the
word that is employed here, and employed so constantly through these Old Testament Scriptures to
describe a peril, and to describe an awful possibility,
we need to recognize the real meaning of the Hebrew
word. Now, shall I very much surprise you if I tell
you that the Hebrew word means quite simply to
mislay ? That is the exact meaning of it. Israel hath
mislaid his Maker. You know what it is to mislay
something. You have not forgotten it, but you have
mislaid it. That is the idea.

Let us examine this carefully. At first blush such
a statement seems to take the sting out of it ; but if
it be carefully considered it will be found that it puts
the sting into it.

To understand this, let us turn aside briefly and look for this Hebrew word *Shâkakh* in other places in the Literature.

When this nation was in the making, when it was coming to national constitution and consciousness, the great God-given leader was Moses. After Moses had led· this people through that tremendous time of constitution, and had been with them for forty years in their wanderings up and down in the wilderness, he was about to leave them ; and taking the Book of Deuteronomy at its face value—and I believe that is the only value—we find in that book his farewell addresses to this very nation.

In these addresses he constantly warned them against one grave peril. What was it ? Forgetting God ; and whenever he did so he used this same Hebrew word. In chapter four, and verse nine, we read :

> " Take heed to thyself, and keep thy soul diligently, lest thou forget the things which thine eyes saw, and lest they depart from thy heart all the days of thy life ; but make them known unto thy children and thy children's children."

That is the meaning of forgetting. Forgetting, is personal neglect of the things that are intellectually believed, and failure to make them the central things of family life. Israel had mislaid God in its individual action, in its national outlook, and in its dealing with its children.

Glance on, and in chapter six, verse ten, we read :

> " And it shall be, when Jehovah thy God shall bring thee into the land which He sware unto

thy fathers, to Abraham, to Isaac, and to Jacob, to give thee ; great and goodly cities, which thou buildedst not, and houses full of all good things, which thou filledst not, and cisterns hewn out, which thou hewedst not, vineyards and olive trees, which thou plantedst not, and thou shalt eat and be full ; then beware lest thou forget Jehovah.''

In other words, When you come into a land where you will be prosperous, said Moses, when you are in the midst of easy prosperity, that dire and disastrous peril to national life and individual life ; beware lest you mislay God.

Yet again ; in chapter eight, and verses eleven and seventeen, we read :

" Beware, lest thou forget Jehovah thy God, in not keeping His commandments, and His ordinances, and His statutes, which I command thee this day ;—And lest thou say in thy heart, My power and the might of my hand hath gotten me this wealth.''

The peril indicated is that of self-satisfaction, which follows when God is mislaid.

And yet once more, in chapter nine, verse one, we read :

" Hear, O Israel ; thou art to pass over Jordan this day.''

Verse four :

" Speak not thou in thine heart, after that Jehovah thy God hath thrust them out from before thee, saying, For my righteousness Jehovah hath brought me in to possess this land . . . not for thy righteousness, nor for thy uprightness of thy heart, dost thou go in to possess their land."

Verse seven :

" Remember, forget thou not."

These are but scattered sentences from these fare-well discourses, but they reveal Moses' sense of the danger of the people. He saw this nation, and he saw it down the coming years, and he knew its supreme peril would be that God should be forgotten. If they could not intellectually forget God, they could put Him out of calculation, they could mislay Him.

From these four quotations we see personal neglect, neglect within the family to train the child ; self-satisfaction that comes from such neglect ; and the self-righteousness which issues, the pride that says, we have made ourselves great ; and finally that terrible mislaying of God which comes from prosperity, which says because of our righteousness and upright-ness of heart God has blessed us, and has given us these things ; and so God is put out of sight, mislaid.

To return to Hosea. The years had run on, centuries had run on, and everything Moses had warned them against had come to pass ; and now this prophet of tears and thunder, as he declared an imminent judgment, said : Here is your malady ; accounting for your transgressions and your trespasses, your false kings and your false princes, your calf in Samaria, your alliance with Assyria, the altars you are building, these are all symptoms. The malady is that you have mislaid God, just mislaid Him, till you have become oblivious of Him. That is the peril of a man, the peril of a nation ; mislaying God.

What is the process ? How do men come to mislay God ? First, they give an intellectual assent to the fact of His existence without seeing to it that their conduct corresponds with their assent. Intellectual orthodoxy will blast a man as surely as heresy will, unless there is the action in life that corresponds with the accurate assent of the mind to truth. That was the story of this nation ; and whenever there is intellectual assent without corresponding action, there is spiritual dullness. God intellectually accepted without response in obedience, fades away from the immediateness of consciousness. He is relegated, it may be, to the temple, and left there ; is relegated, it may be, to the Church on Sunday, and is left there, until we get back next Sunday. If that is so, God help us, we are not Christian. God is mislaid ; He is lost. That was the trouble with Israel. It is the trouble with humanity, God forgotten in that sense ; mislaid, lost as an active power, touching life, conditioning it, inspiring it, driving it, building it up. Israel hath forgotten his Maker.

Well, when that is so, what happens next ? Hosea said Israel was building. Now, if we are looking at the Old Version, it says, " temples " ; the Revised Version says " palaces." Which is right ? They are both right, and they are both wrong. I think either word may be used to convey the sense of the Hebrew word. The word that the prophet made use of literally means " spacious buildings." The old translators said, That means temples. The new translators say, It means palaces. It may mean either ; it may mean both. The true idea is that of spaciousness. Whether that spaciousness was for pleasure or for worship matters nothing. The passion of the nation came to be to build big things. Somebody says these prophets are out of date ! Think again. The passion for bigness is a symptom of capacity for the eternal, for God ; and when men have mislaid God, then they try and build big things without God. Men are ever striving to put back the prison walls, and to build something larger, more spacious. It is manifest supremely to-day on the material level, for all material activity is the symptom of mental and spiritual condition. Great buildings are the order of the day in New York, Chicago, London, everywhere. It is unconsciously symptomatic. Oliver Wendell Holmes in that choice little poem of his, " The Chambered Nautilus," described the nautilus building his own house ever larger, ever larger ; and as he observed it, he wrote the poem, and said in effect that he had learned the secret of life.

" Build thee more stately mansions, O my soul,
   As the swift seasons roll !
   Leave thy low-vaulted past !
   Let each new temple, nobler than the last,
   Shut thee from heaven with a dome more vast,
   Till thou at length are free,
   Leaving thine outgrown shell by life's unresting sea."

That was a great thing. That is humanity's struggle up after the Infinite : " Build thee more stately mansions, O my soul." I am not going to deal with the poem. I would like to say, in passing, it cannot be done. You cannot build more stately mansions for your soul ; and yet the passion is there. It is the passion for the big, the spacious, the infinite, the eternal.

Its expression in the material is tragically futile. Mr. Dooley—one of those magnificent Americans who abound in laughter, and yet are mastered by profound philosophies—wrote an article on machinery. It abounds in merriment, and is full of sanity and sense. At the end of that article he said—I am not quoting the actual words, but the sense of them : We are all busy running round, and building, and putting up, putting up things that are called sky-scrapers by every one, except the sky ! And his last sentence was, " We are still buried by hand."

What an acid satire is there, biting through the rippling humour: We are building sky-scrapers ; we pick up the newspapers and read the descriptions of these vast buildings ; we visit them and go up in the latest of them, and still have to look up to the sky. Sky-scrapers, forsooth !

And yet the passion for the big in humanity is revealed in the building. The prophet says : You have forgotten, you have mislaid God, and you are putting up spacious buildings, sky-scrapers !

Then, as to Judah, he said : She has multiplied fortified cities. If building spacious buildings means the quest for spaciousness, what is the meaning of fortified cities ?

The quest for security, the attempt to secure safety. If the passion for bigness is a symptom of capacity for God, the passion for safety is a symptom of the sense of peril. Safety first ! Have you heard that anywhere ? That is what we are all saying. What does America demand ? What is Britain seeking ? What

does France want ?   What does Italy ask ?   What do
we all want ?   Security.   Security against what ?
I will tell you.   The lack of God, and the things that
result from it.   This great prophet of Israel understood.   We have mislaid God, and now we are building sky-scrapers, and engines of war.   Humanity
forgets God, and then gropes after the spacious, and
fights for the secure, and never makes anything so
big but that the sky laughs at it ; and never secures
itself for one five minutes from a possible outbreak of
devastation.

I said at the beginning that this is a message of
judgment, and so it is.   We cannot turn it into anything else.   How does it end ?   " I will send a fire
upon his cities, and it shall devour the castles thereof."

To forsake God is to ensure ruin.

A fire, what does that mean ?   Does that necessarily
mean that God was about to rain down material fire ?
Oh no.   Away down in Judah, when Hosea was prophesying in the northern kingdom, Isaiah was also
prophesying.   Let us go back to Isaiah, and listen
to something he said one day :

> " The sinners in Zion are afraid ;   trembling
> hath seized the godless ones.   Who among us can
> dwell with the devouring fire ?   Who among us
> can dwell with everlasting burnings ? "

Devouring fire, everlasting burnings ?   What is
that ?—Hell ?   Oh no ; go on, and hear him as he asks
who can dwell in that fire ?   He answers his question :

> " He that walketh righteously, and speaketh
> uprightly ;   he that despiseth the gain of oppres-
> sion, that shaketh his hands from taking a bribe ;

that stoppeth his ears from hearing of blood, and
shutteth his eyes from looking upon evil ; he shall
dwell on high ; his place of defence shall be the
munitions of rocks ; his bread shall be given him ;
his waters shall be sure.   Thine eyes shall see the
King in His beauty."

Who can dwell in fire ?   The pure, those who do not
forget God, who live in right relationship with Him.
If men do forget Him, then that very Divine presence
blasts.   The fire that destroys is the fire of the imman-
ence of God.   We cannot get away from Him.   We
have mislaid Him.   He is at our elbow.   We may be
oblivious of Him, we may do without Him, but all
the while we are living and moving and having our
being in Him.   In His hand our breath is.

And according to our relationship to Him, He will
bless or blast.   If we mislay God, we can run up our
sky-scrapers, we can multiply our battleships ; but
we cannot escape the eremacausis, the slowly burning
fire, which everywhere is purging out the things effete.
We cannot escape God, Who blasts that which forgets
Him by attempting to satisfy the inherent passionate
craving of human life with palaces and dreadnoughts.

VIII

DISTORTED VISION

Hosea ix.

"The prophet is a fool, the man that hath the spirit is mad, for the abundance of thine iniquity, and because the enmity is great."—Hosea ix. 7.

The chapter in its completeness is again a description of calamities which were to overtake Israel because of its pollution. There are five distinct notes sounded as to these calamities ; five elements, shall I say, in the overwhelming calamity that was falling upon the nation that had mislaid its God. The first was the death of joy ; the second, actual exile from their own land ; the third, the loss of spiritual discernment ; the fourth, a falling birth-rate ; and the last, actual casting out.

The text that I have chosen has to do with the central one of these five, namely, the loss of spiritual discernment, and very briefly, by way of introduction to our meditation, I think it is necessary and fair that we refer to the fact that there is admittedly on the part of scholars some obscurity in the text. By that I mean, there are differences of opinion as to what was the simple meaning of the prophet when he uttered the words : " The prophet is a fool, the man of the spirit is mad." Was he then referring to false prophets ?

That is the opinion of Pusey and of George Adam Smith. Or was the prophet describing a false estimate of the prophets held by the people ? That is the opinion of Cheyne and Bullinger.

My own conviction is that Cheyne and Bullinger are right. The prophet Hosea was not here referring to false prophets : " The prophet is a fool, and the man of the spirit is mad." The word " prophet " might have been used for the false prophets. It constantly was so used ; but the phrase, " the man of the spirit," was never used for a false prophet. Hosea is rather declaring the false estimate of the prophet and the man of the spirit which characterized the age that he addressed, and the people to whom his messages were being delivered. This was what men were saying. " The prophet is a fool, and the man of the spirit is mad." Therefore, immediately continuing, he gives the reason for the opinion : " For the abundance of thine iniquity, and because the enmity is great."

Thus, in the text, we are brought face to face with a false conception, and the reason for it. The false conception of the prophetic word, and of spiritual life. " The prophet is a fool." So they were saying. " The man of the spirit is mad." So they were saying. Yes, said Hosea, that is your view, and the reason that you hold that view is to be found in the abundance of your iniquities. and the greatness of your hatred.

Now, leaving all the local colour, we find great principles flash out upon the page, and I invite you to consider these ; first of all this conception of the prophet and the man of the spirit, and then the reason for such conception ; and so finally the delusion of those who hold it.

Centuries have run their course since the times of Hosea, and the conditions of life to-day are, in a thousand and one details, entirely different from the conditions of life then ; but human nature is exactly the same. In the profound and elemental things of human life there is no change. We change the manner of our dress. If you deny that, all you have to do is to get down the family album, and look at your grand-mother's picture ! But you are just the same sort of woman your grandmother was. The elemental things of human nature abide the same through the running centuries. Mothers had broken hearts millenniums ago, as to-day. Youth was exactly what it is ; is exactly what it was. I do not believe the degeneracy of youth to-day is any greater than in the days of my boyhood and youth. To-day it may be more violent in expression ; but then it was more deceitful. Men are still saying, and perhaps with a new insistence and a greater arrogance than they did, the same things ; shall I put it thus ? There is a recurrence of this conception of the prophet and the man of the spirit— " The prophet is a fool, and the man of the spirit is mad."

Let us consider this false conception. " The prophet is a fool." The word there translated fool (*eviyl*) is a somewhat rare one in the Old Testament Scriptures. As a matter of fact it only occurs twenty-five times. There is another word, also rendered " fool " in our versions. For instance, " The fool hath said in his heart." That is not the same word, and the idea is not the same. In the statement, " The fool hath said in his heart there is no God," the word for fool (*nabal*) has a moral element. The reference

is to one degenerate morally.   Such is not the thought
of the text.   I have said it occurs twenty-five times.
It is found only in the Wisdom literature, the poetry,
and the prophetic books.   It occurs twice in the
Book of Job ; only once in the one hundred and fifty
Psalms ; Isaiah, contemporary with Hosea, uses it
twice, and Hosea only once ; and eighteen times in
the Book of Proverbs.

What, then, is the meaning of this word ?   It means
simply inane, or, as we should say, silly—when speaking in contempt.   The prophet is just silly ; daft ;
inane.   The word does not mark immorality in any
sense.   It marks inanity.   The prophet is conceived
of as just a fool, to be dismissed as unworthy of
attention ; beneath contempt.

And " The man of the spirit."   Our rendering gives
it, " The man that hath the spirit " ; but the blunter
reading is, " The man of the spirit."   He is the
spiritual man.   What is the matter with him ?   He is
" mad " ; and here the simple meaning is, he is
" raving."   The man of the spirit, the man of emotion,
the man of force in utterance, the man who is swept
by a conviction until he breaks through all conventionalities, is just raging or raving.

That was the conception that these people had of
Hosea and of Isaiah and of Micah, and of all others
who were uttering to them the words of God, and who,
swept by their own message, consumed by it as by
a fire, violated the conventionalities, broke through
the barriers of supposed accuracy and decency and
orderliness, and flamed in fire and fury against
them.

Let us tarry for a moment to remember the persistence of this conception. I have referred to Isaiah. In chapter twenty-eight of that prophecy we have the account of how he, after a long period of private ministry, which began at the death of Ahaz, broke out into speech in a political situation. The politicians were playing the fool. They were attempting to secure national security by going down to Egypt ; and Isaiah broke out upon them : " Woe to the crown of pride of the drunkards of Ephraim, and to the fading flower of his glorious beauty." Right in the middle of that message we hear these men. They are mocking him ; they are taunting him ; they are laughing at him. At verse nine we have this inter- polation of the mockery of the politicians. What were they saying ? " Whom will he teach knowledge ? and whom will he make to understand the message ? them that are weaned from the milk, and drawn from the breasts ? For it is precept upon precept, precept upon precept ; line upon line, line upon line ; here a little, there a little." They are laughing at him, and what did they mean ? He is just silly ! He is mad ! He is a fool ! Who does he think is going to listen to him ? He has lost his wits !

Later, in the history of Judah, when Shemaiah the false prophet was denouncing Jeremiah, he spoke of him by the very same term. He said, he is just mad.

If we leave those old days, and pass into the New Testament, in the tenth chapter of John we find what His enemies said about Jesus. He is mad, or hath a demon. Read again a little farther on. When Paul was talking to Agrippa, suddenly Festus broke in, and said, " Paul, thou art mad ; thy much learning is turning thee mad."

Or we run on down through the ages ; the Pope said that Luther ought to be in Bedlam ; they charged the Wesleys with madness, drawing from them the retort :

> " Fools and madmen let us be,
> Yet is our sure trust in Thee."

When William Booth broke through the barrier of an ecclesiasticism that was strangling his message, they said, " He is not quite all there " ; and I have heard something very like it said about Billy Sunday. So the conception persists : " The prophet is a fool " ; " The man of the spirit is mad."

Think of these to whom I have thus made reference. Think of Isaiah's message. Remember the magnificence of its dialectics ; the splendour of its rhetoric ; the beauty of its poetry ; and its grasp upon the elemental things of human life. And yet they said that he was a fool, that he was raving.

Listen to the cadences of the heart-broken Jeremiah. He was perhaps the most heroic among all the prophets, in that for over forty years he preached, with no report that he could give statistically that would have been accepted by ecclesiastical courts as being worth while. Yet he thundered forth persistently the message of God to that nation. Consider the marvel of his teaching ; the splendour of his philosophy ; but they said, " He is a plain fool, he is silly, he is mad."

Softly now, and reverently. They said our Lord was mad. Think of His teaching. No more need be said.

They said Paul was mad. I know it has been the fashion in some theological quarters to dismiss him ; but he cannot be dismissed until we have accounted for the wonder of his personality and the marvel of his writings, and the fact that he is seen triumphing through the ages as interpreter of Christ and His Church. And what about Martin Luther ; and William Booth ; and Billy Sunday. Test them by results. And yet of all of them the world said they were mad.

As I survey the whole array, and others I have not named, I am inclined to get Charles Wesley to help me to express myself, and so I repeat his words :

> " Fools and madmen let us be,
> Yet is our sure trust in Thee."

Nevertheless, that is the attitude of the world towards the prophet. His message is accounted silly ; the Word of God, and the prophet's passion of utterance, are accounted mere raving. All of which means the loss of spiritual discernment. The people of Hosea's day had come to that condition. They were turning to Assyria ; they were going to Egypt ; they were consulting wizards ; persisting in pollutions ; to go back upon our previous consideration, they had mislaid God, forgotten God, and they were turning here and there and everywhere ; and when the messenger of God spoke, they said : " The prophet is a fool " ; and when his passion burned with a flame, when there was fury, they said, " The man of the spirit is raving."

And so we turn to consider what the prophet said here as to the reason of this false conception, " Because of the abundance of thine iniquity." The Old Version had it, " The multitude of iniquity." The word suggests the piling up of iniquities. What had that to do with the conception ? Hosea's contemporary, Isaiah, said : " Your iniquities have separated between you and your God." The false conception of the prophet's work, and the false conception of the meaning of the passion of the man of the spirit, were due to blindness with regard to God. This is created by moral declension. That which makes men look upon the messenger of God as a fool, and treat the man of the spirit as mad, is sin.

Consequently, comes the second line of declared reason. Hosea declared that their enmity was great. At the back of the criticism of the prophet and the man of the spirit is hatred. Hatred first of God, and then and therefore, hatred of the messengers of God.

Think of these people! What had happened? Mark the process. They disobeyed God. What next? They forgot Him in the sense of failing to maintain vital relationship with Him : they mislaid Him, and put Him out of their calculations. With what result? They misinterpreted Him. With what result? They hated Him.

The Christian apostle, Paul, speaks of the psychic man. Our Versions render the phrase " the natural man." The Greek word there is *psychic* ; and I think it would be a great gain if we so read it. The man who is merely the man of mentality, the man whose mentality is divorced from spirituality ; the man who is trying to grasp the operations of the universe, but who fails to realize the spiritual element that pervades the universe. Paul says, that man, the merely psychic man, is at enmity against God. Why is it the psychic man is at enmity against God? There is only one reason ; he does not know God, and has a false idea of God. His false idea may be due to his own false philosophy. That old German singer, whose hymns John Wesley translated, expressed a great truth in a couplet, when he sang :

> " O God, of good the unfathomed sea,
> Who would not give his heart to Thee ? "

Why don't men give their hearts to God ? Why don't men reckon with God ? Why do they hate God ? Because they do not know Him. Misapprehension of God is at the root of all hostility to God in the human soul. If I could reveal Him to you, there is neither man nor woman, youth nor maiden, listening to me, who would not be drawn to Him, not one. But the God of our own imagination or interpretation, distant, cruel, vindictive, oftentimes men hate. But that is not God ; that is man's vain imagining concerning Him. This mistaken idea comes of sin, and blindness that has resulted from sin. " Your iniquities have separated between you and your God."

God disobeyed always becomes God distanced from consciousness ; and even when men hold on to some belief in His existence, they are still in revolt, because their conception of Him is false. That is why they call His prophet silly, and the man of the spirit mad.

Let us turn for illustration to a story found in the first Book of the Kings, chapter twenty-two. Ahab was King of Israel, the northern kingdom, and Jehoshaphat King of Judah, the southern kingdom. Ahab an incarnation of wickedness. Jehoshaphat a well-meaning man, without any backbone. These two men were forming an alliance to make themselves safe against the common enemy ; and Jehoshaphat went up and had a meeting with Ahab. The religious undercurrent in Jehoshaphat, and perhaps in Ahab

too, made them feel it was necessary to get some
kind of religious sanction ; and Ahab had arranged a
wonderful gathering. He got prophets of his own
together, and one of them, Zedekiah, the son of
Chenaanah, arranged a very remarkable display. He
put on horns of iron to show how victorious they
were going to be. Jehoshaphat, however, was not
satisfied ; and he had said : " Is there not here a
prophet of Jehovah besides ? " There was one named
Micaiah. Now hear what Ahab said concerning him :
" The King of Israel said unto Jehoshaphat, there is
yet one man by whom we may inquire of Jehovah,
Micaiah, the son of Imlah ; but I hate him." Carefully observe that, " I hate him." Why ? " For he
doth not prophesy good concerning me, but evil."
There was the trouble. The prophet of the Lord will
make no terms with sin. This Ahab knew, and so he
hated him.

So it ever is. The reason for the false conception
is found in the moral turpitude of those who hold the
view. The false conception, so begotten, leads to
hatred. Your iniquity is great, and your enmity is
great.

Now, in conclusion, consider the delusion revealed.
They said " The prophet is a fool." Let us go to that
book in which that word is most often used, eighteen
times. In it we find two definitions of a fool. The
first, " The foolish despise wisdom and instruction " ;
and the second, " Fools make a mock at sin." Thus
the delusion is revealed. The prophet is eternally at
war with sin, and that attitude is the ultimate in
wisdom. Therefore the man that counts him a fool, is
the fool.

The man of the spirit is mad. What is madness ? In experience it is a false view, a lie. Insanity is a false view of life, producing wildness of action and utterance, a pitiable condition. " The man of the spirit is mad," they said. He is mad. He has a false view of life. His utterances are wild and exaggerated, because he fails to understand. Festus said, " Paul, thou art beside thyself ; thou art mad." What did Paul say ? " I am not mad, most excellent Festus ; but speak forth words of truth and soberness." It was Festus who was mad, whose view of life was wrong. His outburst against Paul was the outburst of insanity.

What shall we say of these things considered in the light of all human experience ? First, we declare the rationality of faith. Unbelief is the most irrational attitude possible to man. The man who attempts to account for the things in the midst of which he lives by the things in the midst of which he lives, is bereft of reason. I use the expression carefully ; the rationality of faith. To me it is infinitely more difficult to believe in this world as I see it—I do not mean as man has often spoiled it, but as it is in itself— its mountains and valleys, its oceans and continents, its magnificent splendours, without a God, than with the God of the Bible accounting for it. I cannot believe that the God in Whom I am bound to believe, Who fashioned the daisy and made a man— I care nothing for the moment about the process—is careless about the man, and not interested in him. If I admit God has some care for human life in any way, I cannot believe He is careless about the highest thing in human life which is the moral element and capacity. Faith is utterly rational. To try and account for the things that are by the things that are is to work in a vicious circle. It is the man of faith, the man who endures as seeing Him Who is invisible— mark the contradiction and paradox, and face them —seeing Him Who is invisible, who is the man of rationality. That is the man of reason, that is the man of sanity ; that is the man who is not mad.

Again, I learn as I ponder this message in the light of human life, the inevitableness of passion. One is sometimes tempted to wonder whether people within the Christian Church really do believe the things they say they do believe. I have referred to William Booth, the great founder of the Salvation Army. Do you know what made him the flaming prophet ? He heard an infidel lecturing, and laughing at Christianity. He said : " If I really believed what you Christian people pretend to believe, I would not rest, day nor night, telling men and women about Jesus." William Booth heard it, and it gripped him ; and he said, " The man is right." The result was that he did not rest day nor night.

The Christian Church to-day has largely become—

> " Faultily faultless, icily regular,
>   Splendidly null."

There is very little madness among us. Look at the young Church ; the Church aflame with fire. In its presence the city of Jerusalem said, " These men are drunk." Has any one ever suggested we were drunk because of our Christianity ? If the things we affirm in our creeds are true, we ought to be on fire. The trouble is we are not. They are still saying we are silly, but they do not often say we are mad ; and it is because we have lost—well ! what have we lost ? As God is my witness, I am not arguing for painted fire. It never burns. I am not pleading for a simulated enthusiasm, and never for excitement, which is like the twitching of a galvanized corpse. That is not what I am pleading for. But if we have lost our flame ; if we have lost our fire ; if we have lost our fury, under certain circumstances, against evil; it is because we have lost our vision of God, and we have lost our sense of the greatness of our evangel.

May God restore to us the rationality of faith in fervour, and the passion of enthusiasm that drives us out to do the unusual thing, if necessary, if by any means we may make glad our Lord and our Saviour.

IX

A DEGENERATE VINE

Hosea x.

" Israel is a luxuriant vine, that putteth forth his fruit ; according to the abundance of his fruit he hath multiplied his altars ; according to the goodness of his land they have made goodly pillars. Their heart is divided."—Hosea x. 1, 2a.

Again, chapter ten is a complete message. In the process of the prophecy it concludes a section in which the prophet was dealing with the pollution and the punishment of the people. When we resume at chapter eleven for the remaining chapters, we shall find another note.

The message is of the nature of recapitulation and appeal ; and it opens with the words of our text, in which the whole case is stated as to national failure and its cause. The failure is stated in verse one ; and the cause in that brief sentence which is the opening sentence of verse two. The failure is stated thus, " Israel is a luxuriant vine that putteth forth *his* fruit." That is the story of failure. And the result of the failure is this : " according to the abundance of his fruit he hath multiplied his altars ; according to the goodness of his land they have made goodly pillars." Then the prophet declares in one brief sentence, the all-inclusive cause of failure, " Their heart is divided."

Our meditation will follow these lines ; first, considering the failure as here set forth, of God's ancient people, and the application of the principles to our own times and conditions ; and secondly, considering this startling and yet remarkable revelation of the cause of the failure, " Their heart is divided."

We are at once arrested by the figure of speech which is used. " Israel is a luxuriant vine." The King James Version rendered it, " an empty vine." That is a palpable inaccuracy. It might be rendered an emptying vine. The idea is not that of a vine barren, but of a vine bearing fruit, and that plentifully. Our Revisers have certainly caught the idea far more accurately, as they have it rendered, " Israel is a luxuriant vine."

To us the figure of the vine is familiar, but our familarity with it is principally that of its place in the New Testament, in that marvellous final set discourse of our Lord, uttered to His own disciples immediately before His Cross, which discourse began with the words, " I am the Vine, the true," or as we have rendered it, for the sake of supposed euphony, " I am the true Vine." I prefer to retain the method of the Greek idiom here, with the defining word coming last, sharply, quickly, as our Lord intended it, " I am the Vine, the true." In any case it is that discourse which makes us familiar with the figure.

But it is important to recognize that our Lord was using no new figure of speech ; to the men who heard Him then it was an old and familiar figure. Let us rapidly note the places of its occurrence in the Old Testament. The figure emerges, in the history of the

ancient people, in Psalm eighty, a great Psalm of
Asaph, the leader of the singing.   Asaph was evidently
mourning over some hour of catastrophe in the national
life.   He began :

> " Give ear, O Shepherd of Israel,
>   Thou that leadest Joseph like a flock."

At verse eight he sang :

> " Thou broughtest a vine out of Egypt ;
>   Thou didst drive out the nations, and plantedst it,
> Thou preparedst room before it,
>   And it took deep root and filled the land.
> The mountains were covered with the shadow of it,
>   And the boughs thereof were like cedars of God.
> It sent out its branches unto the sea,
>   And its shoots unto the river."

Then presently he said :

" Look down from heaven, and behold, and visit this vine."

That is the place in the literature, and probably in
the history of these people, where this figure of speech
emerged.   Asaph wrote the music unquestionably for
temple use, and probably wrote the words in this
case also ; and he likened the nation to a vine, the
vine brought out of Egypt and planted.   From that
time on the vine seems to have been the national
symbol.   In the days of our Lord, the great gate of
the Temple, the outer gate, had emblazoned upon it
a golden vine.   It was the symbol of the national
life, a very significant fact when we listen to Jesus
saying, " I am the Vine, the true."

Then when we come to the period of the prophets,
of which Hosea was one, it constantly occurs.

Isaiah, the contemporary of Hosea, employed it in his song of the vineyard, in chapter five.

> " Let me sing for my well-beloved a song of my beloved touching his vineyard. My beloved had a vineyard in a very fruitful hill . . . and he looked that it should bring forth grapes, and it brought forth wild grapes."

Jeremiah, a later prophet, used the same figure of speech, as he described the nation as a " degenerate vine."

Ezekiel, on four or five occasions, used the symbol of the vine, and that in most remarkable ways.

Thus from the time of the kings, and the more ancient history, and through the prophetic period, it was the figure of speech employed as the symbol of national life, and when Hosea said, " Israel is a luxuriant vine," he was employing a familiar figure of speech. If this was a delivered message, when he began, I can imagine that those listening to him were not a little flattered. At first probably they did not detect the method of satire that breathed in his choosing of the figure of speech.

Let us go back for a glance at Isaiah's song. If the figure emerges in Psalm eighty, and is almost constant in the prophetic writings, it is especially interpreted in Isaiah. The opening sentences refer to the vine and the one who planted it ; and then follows the interpretation. I content myself with reading the final verse, verse seven :

> " For the vineyard of Jehovah of hosts is the house of Israel, and the men of Judah His pleasant plant."

Isaiah was a prophet to Judah, and here he was addressing them immediately. " And He looked for justice, but, behold, oppression." The figure says, " He looked for grapes, and it brought forth wild grapes." That is figurative language. What does it mean ? I am not left to speculation. Isaiah interprets. " He looked for justice, He beheld oppression ; for righteousness, but, behold, a cry." That is the interpretation of the figure of the vine. The vine was God's planting. What for ? To bear fruit. What fruit ? Grapes—Justice and righteousness. It brought forth wild grapes. What were they ? Instead of justice, oppression ; and instead of righteousness a cry ; really—although the reading would not be quite euphonistic—a shriek ! That was the national picture. The ideal nation was created by God to bear the fruit of justice and of righteousness for the world. When He sought for fruit He sought for justice, but found its opposite, oppression ; when He sought for righteousness, as a root from which peace and joy must come, He heard a cry, the cry of its iniquity and its suffering, consequent upon its failure.

Now let us return to Hosea's words. " Israel is a luxuriant vine, that putteth forth " what ? " His fruit." This pronoun is not printed with a capital H in the text, and in thinking of it we may think it refers to God. But it is not so. It refers to the nation which is bringing forth its own fruit. The whole emphasis of interpretation and understanding is there. He said Israel is a luxuriant vine, that putteth forth his own fruit, instead of the fruit for which God is looking. The nation was producing fruit, but its own fruit. If, following me patiently, and thoughtfully, and I hope critically examining as I go, some one is inclined to doubt this, then observe what immediately follows :

> " According to the abundance of his fruit he hath multiplied his altars ; according to the goodness of his land they have made goodly pillars."

According to the fruit, the altars ; according to the prosperity of the land, obelisks ; showing at once that the prophet was emphasizing the fact, not of success, but of failure. Israel is a luxuriant vine ; the vine is here. It is bearing fruit, but look at the fruit, and its nature is revealed in the multiplied altars, and the obelisks that are raised everywhere. " Israel is a luxuriant vine, that putteth forth his own fruit." That is exactly what Isaiah was saying in the southern kingdom. He looked for grapes, and behold wild grapes ; He looked for justice, and they had brought forth oppression, wild grapes ; He looked for righteousness, and He heard the cry of the oppressed, and the cry of those in misery.

To summarize then : the charge as here declared is that the nation had failed, in that it was seeking its own interests, instead of the fulfilment of God's purposes.

The words following emphasize the resulting degeneration of religion. According to his fruit, the self-centred seeking of the nation, the altars are built, and they have become the centres of selfishness instead of the symbols and centres of sacrifice. According to the prosperity which is material, they have put up

their pillars, their goodly obelisks ; and the word
" goodly " is a word referring to artistic perfection.
Mark again the irony of it. According to their prosperity they had built themselves ornate idols ; altars
that were no longer the centres and symbols of sacrifice,
but the centres of selfishness. God was lost, mislaid,
and instead of Him there were ornate pillars, obelisks,
stones. That was the degeneration of religion, the
making of religion conform to the low standard of
life. The whole nation forgetting the meaning of its
nationality ; forgetting that it was a vine God had
planted to bear fruit for all peoples ; living a self-
centred life, and in order that the life may be con-
tinued with placidity, religion degenerates ; the altars
are multiplied, and in place of God, ornate idols are
erected.

That day has gone, and the existing conditions have
passed. The local colour has faded from the canvas.
We are living in other times, and under other conditions. But the essential values abide. Let us look
at these.

What does the prophet mean to teach, or shall I
rather say, what does the prophet teach which is
permanent ? That it is possible to prostitute the
resources which God confers upon His people in order
that they might function in the world, for the sake
of the world itself. All those resources may be taken
and consumed upon selfish interests.

Underneath that lies another principle, never to be
forgotten, that the resources of God are always to be
placed at the disposal of men, and that not merely
that men may receive them, but that they also may
be channels, that they may pass on to other men,

and so all men may be reached. The God of the Bible is a missionary God. All the elections of God, of men, of nations, are elections in order that through the men and through the nations so chosen, His beneficent purposes shall reach out to the world. It was because these people came to a false understanding of the doctrine of election that they perished. They came to think of themselves as elected of God—yes, let me say it—to be the pet of God, the pampered of the Most High ; the people that God loved, while He left the rest of the world to drift by. That was the lie that ruined them ; and has robbed them in the world even until this hour of moral and spiritual significance. That is the peril that threatens the Church of God, the forgetfulness of the fact that every benefit is a deposit for which we are responsible, not for self-consumption, but for passing it to others. A luxuriant vine ; the very resources are God's resources, but the fruit is not the fruit for which He is seeking.

Here is an acid test of all life ; an acid test for the individual ; an acid test for the Church ; an acid test for the nation. When in national affairs we make our boast that we are the people of God as amid all people, when we think of the Church as elect of God, when we consider ourselves individually as the recipients of God's favour, let us never forget the reason of the choice, the election, the favour. If God has created us a nation, it is in order that through us the breadth and beauty and beneficence of the Divine government may be revealed and administered to all peoples. If God has created the nation, the fruits He desires, what are they ? Justice and righteousness. If He finds oppression, and if He hears a cry, then the nation may be a luxuriant vine, but it is bringing forth its own fruit, and so is a disastrous failure.

The same is true in application to the Church. What are we after ? What is our purpose ? What is our passion ? What do we want ? What are we supremely trying to do ? What is our goal, our aim, our objective ? Should any one say, " we are seeking the crowds," the next question is, what for ? Why do we want to see our congregations increase in our Churches, and the people flocking to our doors ?

In that is involved yet another question. How are we seeking to attract them ? Our passion to-day is for efficiency. Splendid. But still we ask, efficient for what ?

Let us yet ask another question. What is the result of all our activity, of the multiplication of agencies and associations and committees and Synods and Sessions and groups, and what-nots ? What is the issue ? I am not answering my question. I am asking it. Is it justice ? Is the result of our life and our activity justice ? Or are we still condoning oppression ? Is the result of all our service righteousness ? Or does God hear a cry ?

I said that the word may be rendered " a shriek." The word is very remarkable. Let me give you two illustrations of its use. It occurs first in Genesis eighteen, when it is said that God heard the cry of Sodom and Gomorrah. It is the same word in Exodus, when God heard the cry of the oppressed people coming up from Egypt. So the word may be used to mark a condition of sin or of suffering ; but wherever, listening, one hears the howling of the sinner, or the wailing of sorrow, we know conditions contrary to His mind, contrary to His will.

The question is vital, is the Church in her activity to-day bearing the fruit for which God is seeking ? The acid test of any Church's life is that of her passion, that of her purpose ; and ultimately, that of her results. If the passion be merely for a crowd, if the passion be merely for organic efficiency, then all sorts of things fasten on to the life of the Church, parasitic growths, sapping energy, contributing nothing to her value in the world. The Church is cursed to-day with fungus growths, all sorts of institutions, until one hears constantly the click of machinery ; and then we look for fruit, and the supreme question is what the fruit is, that of the Divine intention, or that of our selfishness. A people God-made may be a luxuriant vine, may be spreading forth their branches, and yet failing to function according to the Divine purpose.

Now consider what the prophet says happens. This again is a startling thing. He does not say these things result from altars and obelisks. He says altars and obelisks result from these things. " Israel is a luxuriant vine, that putteth forth his fruit ; according to the abundance of his fruit he hath multiplied his altars." The deficiency in the religious life of the nation resulted in the multiplication of altars, because the nation had to adapt its religion to conform to its failure. The altars were ornate and artistic ; but no sacrifice was inspired by them. They put up obelisks, as I have said, ornate altars instead of God ; stone, passivity instead of passion, for passivity and passion mean the exact opposite. We see the obelisks all through the land, highly carved and beautiful, and æsthetic pillars, rising in their stately glory, shall I say splendour ? Yes, if I may, but another word is needed—impotence ; stone instead of bread ; passivity instead of passion ; human artistry instead of Divine beauty. What is the difference between the beauty of God and human artistry ? Where do we see the beauty of God most perfectly ? Do we see it in the star-bespangled heavens ? No. In the wonders of Nature, as we observe them in the infinitely small and the great ? No. Where do we see it most perfectly ? In the wounded and mutilated Man of the Cross. That is beauty. To the Greek with his passion for so-called culture and refinement, and everything that is æsthetic, it was ugliness. A mutilated man is an offence to beauty, says the Greek. But we know full well that all Heaven's beauty shines in the way of the Cross. Every man or woman who is twisted and maimed and disfigured for life, through sacrifice and service, has a beauty not to be found in the Art which despises disfiguration. In the Song of Solomon, the Shulammite says at one point,

> " They made me keeper of the vineyards ;
> But mine own vineyard have I not kept."

She was not complaining. She was glorying in the fact that she had lost her complexion in service. Talking to the women of the court in the marvellous idyllic poetry, she said in effect : It is quite true, I have been out in the fields, and I have lost my complexion. That is what she meant by " I am black, but I am comely." There is beauty in a marred face when it is marred in the service of others. Things of artistic refinement, goodly obelisks ; things of æsthetic beauty, instead of the God of the Cross ; things of human artistry instead of Divine beauty ; and the inevitable result, a degraded people.

Gather it all up and express it in a sentence or two. A people God-created, God-planted ; a people intended to function for God in the interests of humanity at large ; a vine planted by God to bring forth the fruit of justice and righteousness ; the vine is still existing, the branches are spreading ; and the statistics seem to be satisfactory, and yet, there may be no fruit that satisfies the passion of God. If that is so, religion degenerates, altars record no sacrifice ; the symbols of selfishness replace God. The worship of the artistic according to human thinking, and the relegation of the religion of the Cross into the background as something vulgar, is ever the degeneration of religion.

Then in a short, sharp, arresting sentence Hosea reveals the reason for the failure ; " Their heart is divided." The word rendered " heart," and so constantly used in the Old Testament, means something which is enclosed. Physically it refers to the innermost organ of the body, which is the centre of action and life. Figuratively it is employed sometimes as referring to feelings, sometimes as referring to the intellect, and sometimes as referring to the will. It is most often used as referring to the sum totality of personality. In this case it is used without any question as referring to the central realm of personality, the realm of desire. The heart divided !

We are arrested, and at first almost startled by this word " divided." Not the English word, but the Hebrew word *Chalaq*. It means smooth. In what sense, or how can that mean " divided " ? They came to use that word for divided, because it applied to the smooth stones with which they cast lots. Sometimes we say in England, a man is dicing his inheritance away. We have taken the word dicing from the instrument of gambling. They used smooth stones, with which they cast lots in dividing. Divided, smooth, casting lots.

In the central realm of personality, the realm of desire, they were casting lots, gambling with God, playing God off against something else, playing something else off against God, flinging dice in the centre of personality. Their heart was a gambling-house.

Or to return to our common use of the word divided. One of the ancient psalmists prayed a prayer, and what a prayer it was. He said, " Unite my heart to fear Thy name." Jeremiah uttering the word of God said to the people, " I will give them one heart, and one way, that they may fear Me for ever, for the good of them, and of their children after them." It is the divided heart which causes the trouble. When into the realm of desire we allow God and something else to enter and compete for mastery, that is the story of all failure. We begin by wanting God and something else, and presently we want something else and God ; and God will not be there on those terms. Consequently we eliminate Him, we mislay Him ; and when He is mislaid the vine remains, but the fruit changes. Instead of the grapes, wild grapes, acrid, acid, poisonous, destructive ; instead of justice, oppression ; instead of righteousness, a cry ; and all because the heart is divided.

Let us end the meditation by grouping some words scattered across the Bible. Again a psalmist is speaking : " One thing have I desired of the Lord, that will I seek after, that I may dwell in the house of the Lord for ever." One thing. Jesus is speaking to a rich young ruler, " One thing thou lackest." Jesus is speaking to a woman cumbered with caring about things, " One thing is needful." A little way on, a great soul says, " One thing I do, forgetting the things behind, I press towards the mark." One thing, one thing, one thing ! Some one says, " I should not like to be a man of one idea." Why not ? It depends upon your idea. If your idea is big enough you have not room for more than one. If the one idea be to dwell in the house of the Lord ; if the one idea be to render absolute allegiance to Him and follow His Christ ; if the one idea is to be so completely under His domination to fulfil His purpose ; if the one idea is to reach the goal, to fulfil His purpose, and to be His instrument of blessing ; you do not want two ideas. The trouble with us is that the passion for variety puts God in a list with other things. That is the divided heart. We need to pray in our own hearts, " Unite my heart to serve Thee, O God."

X

THE COMPASSION OF GOD

HOSEA xi.–xii. I

" How shall I give thee up, Ephraim ? how shall I cast
thee off, Israel ? how shall I make thee as Admah ? how
shall I set thee as Zeboiim ? My heart is turned within
Me, My compassions are kindled together."—HOSEA xi. 8.

HERE begins the last movement in the prophecy of
Hosea. In these last four chapters the emphasis is
upon one note, that of the love of God. Hosea,
prophesying in the dark days of the declension and
backsliding of the northern kingdom of Israel, had
been brought into fellowship with God through tragedy
in his own home, through which tragedy, the tragedy
of wounded love, there had come to him an understanding of the Divine heart. This has been realized
throughout, but in this last movement it comes into
special prominence.

So far we have been considering different points in
the process of that ministry of stern denunciation,
and have heard the prophet's constant call to these
people to return to God. Now in the last four chapters
the dominant note is that of the love of God. As I
have said, it has not been absent from any part of
the prophesying ; but as it comes to climacteric con-

clusion, the great and wonderful emphasis of the message is laid upon that love.

The literary method of these chapters is arresting. A remarkable alternation runs through them. The prophet speaks as God, that is, as the mouthpiece of God, Jehovah speaks through him; and then he speaks for himself. Of course what he says himself is under guidance, but there is a distinct alternation. We hear the voice of Jehovah, and then the voice of the prophet.

Let us observe the movement through. There are four speeches of Hosea as the mouthpiece of Jehovah; and three times the prophet breaks in with his own comments. The interpolations of the prophet are all in the minor key; and those he speaks for Jehovah are all in the major key, declaring the triumph of love. There is no disagreement between Jehovah and the prophet; but the mental mood of Hosea is revealed. He is still delivering the message of Jehovah; but evidently amazed that any such message could be delivered, for in his three interpolations he confesses the sin of the people. God is telling of His love, and the prophet amazed at it, breaks in, and describes the sin of the people.

To indicate the alternation. The speech of Jehovah begins in chapter eleven, and runs through to the end of the first verse in chapter twelve. Then suddenly the prophet speaks for himself, beginning at the second verse of chapter twelve, and running to the end of verse six. Again, from verse seven in chapter twelve to verse eleven Jehovah speaks. Once more, at the twelfth verse, and running through to the first verse of the next chapter, thirteen, Hosea is the speaker.

At the second verse of chapter thirteen Jehovah
resumes, and His words continue to the end of verse
fourteen. Then at the fifteenth verse of chapter
thirteen, and as far as the third verse of chapter
fourteen, the prophet is again heard. Everything
ends, beginning at the fourth verse of chapter fourteen, and running to the end, with the voice of
Jehovah.

Thus the alternation. Jehovah speaks, and the
prophet speaks ; Jehovah continues, the prophet
continues ; Jehovah speaks, and the prophet speaks ;
and all ends with the speech of Jehovah. Throughout,
the speech of Jehovah is burdened with love ; and
the messages of the prophet are burdened with a sense
of the unworthiness of the people. We are conscious
of the major music of the Divine love, and the minor
threnody of Hosea's sense of sin.

The message beginning with chapter eleven, and
ending with the first verse of chapter twelve, is vibrant
with love. Jehovah, speaking of these people, rebellious, renegade, tells of His love for them ; goes
back and speaks of the love that was His at the very
beginning of their history, traces the course and
activity of that love through that history ; and in our
text breaks out into this cry,

> " How shall I give thee up, Ephraim ? how
> shall I cast thee off, Israel ? how shall I make
> thee as Admah ? how shall I set thee as Zeboiim ?
> My heart is turned within Me, My compassions
> are kindled together."

In these words we have four questions. There is,

however, a little difference in the Hebrew form. We read,

> " How shall I give thee up, Ephraim ? How shall I cast thee off, Israel ? "

The second " how " is not there in the Hebrew. Again,

> " How shall I make thee as Admah? How shall I set thee as Zeboiim ? "

and the second " how " in that couplet is not here in the Hebrew. They have been supplied by translators for the sake of euphony ; and again I am not quite sure that the change is helpful. This is how it runs in the Hebrew :

> " How shall I give thee up, Ephraim ? shall I surrender thee, O Israel ? "

That is the first couplet.

> " How shall I make thee as Admah ? Shall I set thee as Zeboiim ? "

That is the second couplet.

Admah and Zeboiim were the cities of the plain that were destroyed when Sodom and Gomorrah were destroyed. The prophet does not name the major cities, for reasons not now to be discussed.

" How shall I make thee as Admah ? " as that blackened city of the plain that was destroyed. " Shall I set thee as Zeboiim ? " another of the cities swept

out because of its iniquities. Then comes the great
answer :

> " My heart is turned within Me, My com-
> passions are kindled together."

So much for the technical setting of the text.

Let us ponder, first, the surprising nature of these
questions ; secondly, the explanation of them ; and
thirdly, the answer as declared.

The surprising nature of the questions is at once
seen if we remember the Speaker, and those of whom
He was speaking. Throughout, Jehovah is heard
emphasizing Himself. In my Bible I have put a little
red ring round every capital " I " Let me read the
brief sentences introduced by that repeated " I."

First the affirmations :

> " I loved him . . . I taught Ephraim to walk
> . . . I nursed them . . . I healed them. I drew
> them with the cords of love . . . I lifted the
> yoke . . . I fed them. . . ."

Then the questions :

> " How shall I give thee up ? " . . .

Finally the declarations .

> " I will not .   . I will not . . . I am God . . .
> the Holy One . . . I will not . . . I will not . . .
> I will make them dwell."

That is very mechanical, but it gives us a vision of
God. Notice the amazing merging of the figures of

speech which are found in those words which God spoke about that people. First we find the Father :

> " When Israel was a child, then I loved him, and called My Son out of Egypt."
> " I taught Ephraim to walk."
> " I took them on My arms."

That is, I was a Nurse to them.

> " I healed them."

Fatherhood and Motherhood are there. Loving, teaching to walk, nursing, healing.

Then we find another figure of speech. No longer the Father, but the husband.

> " I drew them with the cords of a man, and bands of love."

That can only be understood as we remember the first part of the prophecy. Hosea knew what that meant. He had been commanded to go and love a woman who had broken his heart, and take her back home again. Jehovah thus spoke under the figure of a husband :

> " I drew them with the cords of a man." " I drew them with bands of love."

Then perhaps the most startling figure emerges.

> " I was to them as they that lift up the yoke on their jaws ; and I laid food before them."

In these words Jehovah describes Himself as a Herdsman. It is a picture of the cattle coming home at night, after the toil of the wearisome day : I lifted the yoke, and freed their jaws, and fed them ! Thus

Jehovah reveals Himself all the way through ; the Father, the Husband, and the Herdsman.

Now look again at the people as described. Four little sentences cover the ground. They went from Me ; they did not know that I was healing them ; they refused to return ; they are bent on backsliding.

Thus the contrast of persons and actions is vivid. Jehovah is seen as the persistent Lover, and the people as contemning His love. What is to be done ? There is only one thing to do, by all the laws of human conduct, and all the laws that are only laws of righteousness and equity and justice. Give them up, abandon them. If in some hearts there is a protest against that statement, I ask where was that protest born ? What is the inspiration of the feeling that it is not necessary to abandon them ? I declare that when I see the Lover, teaching to walk, nursing with a tender care, healing ; Father, Husband, Herdsman ; and then watch these people definitely, persistently, positively rebellious ; I say there is only one thing to do with them : give them up. And yet there is a protest against that view. I repeat my question —why should there be such a protest ? We never would protest if we did not know something about this God. Some of the by-products of Christianity are the most marvellous things in human life. Go anywhere else than to the lands in which the light of this God has streamed upon men, and wrought results far wider than any of our statistics can show ; go to any civilization in the past or the present, and tell this story, and apart from the revelation of God that has come to us, and changed our whole outlook on life, we shall say, There is nothing to do with people like that, but to give them up.

Here, then, we are face to face with something surprising. Jehovah says, " How can I give thee up ? " They have left Me. They do not know Me, and this in spite of all I am doing for them. I have sent the prophets to them, but they refused to return. They are bent on backsliding. It is all true, but " how can I give them up ? "

There was something holding Jehovah back from judgment ; and whatever it was, it was something that won, for we hear words three times repeated, " I will not . . . I will not . . . I will not." I loved from childhood, and taught to walk, took them on My arms, healed them, drew them back, fed them ; and they turned their back upon Me, and they are going on turning their back upon Me ; they are bent on backsliding ; but " how can I give thee up ? I will not . . . I will not . . . I will not."

What, then, was it holding Him back ? The answer is in the text :

> " My heart is turned within Me, My compassions are kindled together."

Was it something in Israel that made God say, " How can I give thee up ? " ? As I look at Israel I should say, Surely not. It was not something in Israel, but something in God. And yet, the something in God saw in Israel possibilities that I cannot see, that seem to have faded, seem to have been obliterated. He saw them. He always does. God always sees the possibility of human life. That is the meaning of the Cross. Whatever we may think about human nature,

God thought it worth dying for. He saw the possibility. He saw what Israel might be, what the boy He loved and called out of Egypt and nursed and fed might be. I cannot see it as I look at them, can you ? As God is my witness, I cannot see it when I look at myself. That is the amazing thing. Because of what God is, He sees me, and sees my possibility ; and in spite of all my backsliding, in spite of all my disobedience, in spite of the fact that I have contemned His love, He is saying :

> " I cannot give you up. I will not, I will not, I will not ! "

The secret of it is found in the words, " My heart is turned within Me." That is a very expressive word. Turned about, or turned over, literally ; but in use it is the word that describes upheaval, turmoil. Listen. God says My heart is in turmoil ; My heart is moved to its depths, My heart ! Again, " My compassions are kindled together," and the word " compassion " there does not mean sorrow, it does not mean pity. I think sometimes in our own language there is only one word that accurately can carry over its meaning. It means solace ; and that means more than power to solace, but solace in activity. It is more than pity and sorrow. It is pity and sorrow in action. " My compassions are kindled." Strange word that. If we go back to the eighth chapter, and the fifth verse, we read,

> " He hath cast off thy calf, O Samaria ; Mine anger is kindled against them."

Now He says, " My compassion is kindled." It is not the same word, though. " My compassions are *kindled*,"

that is, are deeply affected ; " Mine anger is kindled,"
that is, caused to glow. The word " kindled " used
concerning His compassions means quite literally
" contracted." " My compassions are contracted."
This, however, not in the sense of narrowed ; but
rather My compassions are in spasm, deeply affected.
Somebody says that is all anthropomorphic, speaking
of God under human figures. I am not denying it ;
it is so, but there is no other presentation possible.
How are you to grasp God save as you think of Him
as He tells you to think of Him, as a Man. The
Incarnation is God's final Self-interpretation, the
Speech of Himself to man in the terms of humanity,
that man may grasp the truth concerning Deity.
Here, then, employing the human, Jehovah declares
that He is in turmoil. " My compassions are kindled."
That is why He cannot give them up. Here we are
in the presence of Love, love that is not the mere
sentimental outgoing of an emotional nature, evanescent and passing ; but love that becomes an agony ;
love that becomes a tragedy. Faber was right :

> " There is no place where earth's sorrows
> Are more felt than up in heaven."

John Watson, better known as Ian Maclaren, the
author of *The Bonnie Brier Bush*, once said, " God is
the chief Sufferer in the universe." He was right.
This is the suffering God, and it is God suffering
because of His love ; and it is love in agony not because those He loves are wronging Him, but wronging
themselves, and blighting themselves, and blasting
themselves. How, being what I am, says God, can I
give you up ?

And yet do not forget that the " how " suggests the difficulty. How can I give thee up ? Justice alone says it is the right thing that the rebellious shall be punished ; but how can I do it ? And that compassion led to the decision, " I will not."

Now quietly for a moment or two. How came it that God could say " I will not " ? Let us listen.

> " I will not execute the fierceness of Mine anger, I will not return to destroy Ephraim ; for I am God, and not man, The Holy One in the midst of thee."

Here, all mere intellectuality breaks down ; here is something very strange. I have been talking about His love. He has spoken of a heart in turmoil, of compassions that are moved to the very depths, and He says I will not give you up ; what is the reason ? Because of His heart and His compassions ? Yes, but go on. " I am God, and not man," and I am " the Holy One in the midst of thee." There is no lowering of the standard of moral requirement. The Holy One can be compassionate and remain holy because He is God, and not man. Things are possible to Him that are not possible to man.

That is as far as we get in Hosea. It is a long way, but it leaves us asking questions ; and filled with wonder, we do not understand it. It is as though, on this page, and through all the Old Testament, the glory is breaking through, but never coming into clear manifestation. A wonder and a mystery of righteousness and compassion are seen working together. Wonderful seeing was the seeing of the prophet who could write a thing like that. That must have come by inspiration, or else it is the fairest mirage that ever deceived the heart of humanity. When God, in spite of sin, says, How can I give you up ? My heart is stirred, My compassions are stirred, but I am holy ; how can I give you up ? and yet says, I will not give you up, I will not, I will not, we are in the presence of some possibility wholly of God. It must have been a great word for trembling and troubled hearts even then.

But our Bible does not end in Hosea. The name Hosea meant salvation. I do not know who named him. The father or mother, or both, in all probability ; but they called that boy Hosea, a sob and sigh and song merging in a name. There came One in the fulness of time, whose Name was Jehovah and Hosea : Jesus. So in the fulness of time the gleams and glints of glory broke out into full manifestation ; and we find out at last in Jesus, how God can be just, and the Justifier of the sinning soul.

This way of accomplishment Hosea did not see. In communion with God he had learned facts about the Divine Nature which seemed to be conflicting, and he delivered his message and uttered the words ; but at last He came, Who is the Brightness of the Father's glory and the express Image of His Person, and in Him I see how righteousness and peace meet together, and God can be just and the Justifier.

Through Him the claims of justice which are against my soul are all met. Through Him the glory of holiness is maintained ; for His redemption of the human soul is not a pity that agrees to ignore sin ; but a power that cancels it and sets free from its dominion. Through Him the loved one is regained, restored, renewed, and all the lights that flash and gleam upon the prophetic page, astonishing my soul, come into focused unity in Jesus. God says of you, of me, " How can I give thee up ? I will not . . . I will not . . . I will not."

But how ? " I am God and not man, I am the Holy One." Through Christ He has made the way by which sinning souls can be conformed to His image, His likeness, His will. The Gospel is gleaming in Hosea. It is shining in full radiance in Christ.

We can leave the historic and come to the immediate. That is God. But in order to provide ransom, and redemption, and renewal, what ? The answer is found fully in the words :

> " God so loved the world that He gave His only begotten Son, that whosoever believeth in Him should not perish, but have everlasting life."

XI

ISRAEL BECOME CANAAN

HOSEA xii. 2–xiii. 1

" He is a trafficker."—HOSEA xii. 7.

THESE are again the words of Jehovah. Chapter
eleven, to the end of the first verse of chapter twelve,
which we read in connection with our last meditation,
was wholly the speech of Jehovah. Then, in the
present reading, in verses two to six, the prophet is
speaking. His words constitute an interpolation, by
no means out of harmony with the general tenor of
the revelation, but one in which he speaks of the
history of these people. He goes back to the birth
of Jacob, refers to it, and then refers to his experience
at Peniel, when he became Israel, the night when he
contended with God and gained a victory, not by
strength, but by weakness, when with sobs and tears
and cries pouring out of his soul, he prevailed, after
which his name was no more to be Yawkob, heel-
snatcher, but Israel, a man ruled by God.

Then at verse seven the Speaker is once more
Jehovah. The prophet resumes his rôle as the mouthpiece of Jehovah, and breaks in with the words :

" He is a trafficker, the balances of deceit are
in his hands : he loveth to oppress."

The words of Jehovah break in upon the prophet's words, upon his interpretation of the past, especially his reference to the night in which this man became Israel. The prophet was thinking of the night by the Jabbok, when Jacob became Israel, and as he refers to it, Jehovah breaks in : " He is a trafficker."

Our Versions vary in translation here. The King James Version renders it : " He is a merchant," with a marginal reading, " Or, Canaan." The English Revision renders it: " He is a trafficker," with a marginal reading, " Or, a Canaanite. Heb. Canaan." The American Standard Version renders it : " He is a trafficker," with a marginal reading, " Or, a Canaan-ite. Heb. Canaan." Thus the Revisers, English and American, agree. The difference between the older rendering and the newer is merely one of attitude towards the idea. The old translators dignified it by using the word " merchant." Our translators em-ployed a word which may mean the same thing, but has in it an ugly suggestion—" trafficker." Of which, more presently.

Look again at the Translations. In each of them we find the words, " He is." Now, I admit that there are times when translators are compelled to introduce some words, not actually found in the text, by reason of the idiom of a language. This is what they have done here. There is no " He is " in the Hebrew. As a matter of fact, there is only one word, " Canaan." This is suggested in each marginal reading. It is an abrupt and contemptuous word.

Now that may be a somewhat startling thing to say, because we very often make Canaan refer to

heaven. We sing about Canaan's happy land, and
all sorts of other stupid things. Our idea has been
that the wilderness represents this world, and Canaan
represents heaven ; and so we sing :

> " Could I but climb where Moses stood,
> And view the landscape o'er,
> Not Jordan's flood, nor death's cold stream,
> Should fright me from the shore."

The idea is utterly unscriptural. The wilderness is
not a type of what our life on earth should be. Canaan
is not a type of heaven. If Canaan is a type of heaven,
then the first work we shall have to do when we reach
heaven is to drive out the Hivites and the Jebusites
and the Perizzites ! That is not heaven. Yet, with
that false idea of Canaan as a heavenly land, the land
that lies beyond, we are in danger of missing the
suggestiveness of the word as used by Jehovah here.
Therefore let us examine the matter carefully.

The prophet had listened in wonder to the love-
song of Jehovah, " When Israel was a child then I
loved him . . . called My Son out of Egypt," and
had turned aside to the birth of Jacob, when he was
a heel-snatcher ; and then had remembered the moment
when he ceased to be a heel-snatcher, and became
Israel ; and he gloried in the idea of Israel. Then God
suddenly broke across his meditations, and said
" Canaan."

Now we may insert a verb, but when we translate
the noun " merchant " or " trafficker," we are missing
something. Let it stand as " Canaan." That word
stands all the way through the Old Testament literature with one significance, and it is that of complete

contrast with what is suggested by the word" Israel."
The two words constitute the most striking an-
tithesis.

Let us then consider this matter, first in the story
of these peoples, and in its revelation of abiding
principles.

To treat the word Canaan as a synonym for a
merchant is understandable, but it is wrong. I admit
that the word Canaan had acquired that meaning, and
was often used in that way. But that is not the
meaning of the Hebrew word in itself. It was, as I
have said, acquired, just as the word Chaldean acquired
the suggestiveness of astrology, simply because
astrology flourished in Chaldea. All the Chaldeans
were not astrologers, and Chaldean never strictly
meant astrologer. Dr. Kyle points out with great
lucidity that Canaan acquired the sense of merchant-
man as Chaldean acquired the sense of astrologer.
Canaan never really meant merchant-man, as Chaldean
never really meant astrologer. The Hebrew word
literally means " humiliated."

In the Bible literature Canaan emerges in Genesis,
chapters nine and ten, in the story of Ham. From
there throughout Biblical history the intention of the
word harmonizes with its use at that point. It is a
word always used to describe a people humiliated on
account of depravity. Canaan means quite literally,
subjugated, humiliated ; but it always connotes the
humiliation of depravity, pollution. Therefore in the
Biblical literature Canaan is always the synonym for
corruption, the degradation of a people which results
from their pollution, which in turn results from the
fact that they have lost contact with God.

Now turn to Israel, and consider its relation to Canaan in the Divine Economy. What did God mean when He put Israel in Canaan ? That raises a question which brings us into the realm of a difficulty in the minds of many who declare that they do not believe that God was the Author of war against the Canaanites. For myself, I may at once say that if I did not believe God would make war against what is revealed concerning Canaan, I could not believe in God at all ! The reason for the attitude of God towards these Canaanites is explicitly stated in the Book of Leviticus :

> " Defile not ye yourselves in any of these things ; for in all these the nations are defiled which I cast out from before you ; and the land is defiled ; therefore I do visit the iniquity thereof upon it, and the land vomiteth out her inhabitants. Ye therefore shall keep My statutes and Mine ordinances, and shall not do any of these abominations ; neither the home-born, nor the stranger that sojourneth among you (for all these abominations have the men of the land done, that were before you, and the land is defiled)."

If any one desires fuller details concerning the conditions of these people, let him take up the study of archæology. The revelation is appalling. Israel was raised up, and sent into that land to cleanse a plague spot, which was blasting the whole world by its influence. Jehovah is a Man of war, against everything that blights and blasts humanity. When humanity will not listen to the gentle wooing of His love, then, with the skill of the surgeon, He cuts the

cancer out. That is not love, which stands by any
individual sufferer from some terrible malady which
is curable by excision, and quotes poetry and attempts
to soothe the sufferer. God is not a God of such
methods. He sent Israel into Canaan to cut the
cancer out, to free the region from the degraded,
depraved people, whose abominations are revealed in
the tablets we are finding to-day, corroborating the
Divine story.

He put them there also in order to plant in that
little land, central to the whole earth, a centre of
health, to dry up the poisoned streams, that there
might issue forth the streams of purity and grace to
bless the whole world.

Strategically, Palestine is the geographical centre
of this globe. Think of the continents of the earth
circling round it. There was a time when the Medi-
terranean Sea was the centre of everything ; and then
the centre moved to the Atlantic Ocean. It is now
leaving the Atlantic Ocean, and moving out to the
Pacific Ocean. The great problems of to-day are
centred there. I believe that the movement will
sweep over the intervening lands and come back to
the same land some day.

Be all that as it may, Canaan then was corrupt,
rotten through and through ; and the Divine movement was that of cleansing out a corrupt people, and
placing there a people separate, clean, pure. God put
them there, to cut out a plague spot, and to create a
centre of health for all the nations.

Now listen to the text. God said of that people—
Canaan !—Israel was created to make Canaan Israel.
The time had come when Canaan had made Israel

Canaan. The Divine purpose was that Israel, a people God-governed, should go into the Canaan of degeneracy and subjugation to everything impure, that humiliated and depraved country, not in its own estimation, but in its moral condition, and turn it into a God-ruled place and people—Israel. The years had run on, and instead of Israel making Canaan Israel, Canaan had made Israel into Canaan. The ejaculation of a name was therefore the most terrific indictment. " Canaan ! " said God. The prophet remembering the birth of Jacob, the prophet remembering the night by the Jabbok, the prophet remembering how the man became Israel, and his soul thinking of the issue ; then he stopped ; and God broke in, and said " Canaan ! "

The principles revealed are sun-clear. The first and self-evident is that God's elections are always in the interests of humanity. That cannot be over-emphasized. It cannot too often be stated. It is one of the things that the subtlety of the human heart is constantly in danger of forgetting, and it is one of the things of which those who are the elect of God, His selected servants, are always in danger of losing sight. And yet the whole revelation of the Bible is the revelation of that fact. Let me repeat the words of my statement. God's elections are always in the interests of humanity. God's elections are always in order to inclusion, and never to exclusion. If He elects, it is not that He may exclude others, but that He may elect those through whom the others shall presently be included. If we take Bible history, we can write over and of it, " God so loved the world." If He chooses Abraham, He says to Abraham, " I will

bless thee, and make thee a blessing ; I will make of
thee a great nation, in order that all nations shall be
blessed in thee." If He creates the nation of Israel,
He does it in order that Israel shall be the centre from
which light shall flash out to the other nations, that
they may no longer walk in the darkness, in order
that streams of health morally may proceed throughout the world. Elections are always in the interests
of the world. Softly and reverently, not to put this
Name into comparison, but to recognize it as higher
than all possibility of comparison. Jesus was the
Elect, the Anointed, the Chosen, the Messiah. Why ?
" God so loved the world that He gave His only
begotten Son, that whosoever believeth in Him should
not perish, but have everlasting life." The Church
is not an end, it is a means to an end. The Church is
not a nation of spiritual privilege, which God has
created that He may lavish His love upon it, while
He lets the rest of the world drift to darkness and dis-
order. The Church is the instrument through which
He would reach the world.

To recognize this principle is to understand the
sudden, majestic, and terrific word with which
God broke across the words of the prophet, and
said " Canaan !" It is the severest indictment
possible.

The second principle is involved in the first. If
God's elections are always in the interests of humanity,
it follows that the chosen instrument must be true to
the Divine purpose, and to the Divine standards. It
cannot compromise with evil, and fulfil its Divine
commission. If Israel be contaminated by Canaan,
Israel cannot influence Canaan towards its own ideals,

or the God Who governs them. The chosen instrument must for evermore be true to the Divine purpose for which it was created, and to the Divine standards by which it is called to live.

Therefore, finally, it is seen that the enterprise of God in the world must always be one of conflict during the period of process, till Israel changes Canaan, or Canaan changes Israel. Either the Church will influence the world, by attracting her to her Lord, declaring His evangel, proclaiming His ethic ; either the Church is encroaching upon the territory of the world, and bringing it under the rule of God ; or else the world is affecting the Church, weakening her, robbing her of her testimony and power. There is always a conflict. The terrible thing is, that as God said of His ancient people on this occasion—Canaan— it may be that He has to say the same thing sometimes of His Church—the World ! I fear it must be admitted that there are places and Churches where it would be very difficult for a man to find the difference between the Church and the world. The line of demarcation has been almost blotted out in many cases. The things that distinguished the Church from the world in her early stages, when she had to stand up against the dark pagan world, upon which deep lust and loathing fell, are largely lost. The very genius of her life is such as to bring her into unceasing conflict with the powers of darkness. The absence of that conflict to-day is ominous. It seems to me that of many God must be saying, I made a Church to bless the world, and the Church is hardly distinguishable from the world.

The application of this meditation to the Church

is clearly found in one paragraph in the New Testament. In the earlier period of the Christian emprise, when the man apprehended by Jesus on the Damascene road, Paul, was engaged as the pioneer missionary and messenger of the Cross, he lighted upon the city of Corinth, and he planted the Church there ; and presently as he passed on, another came, Apollos, and he watered. After awhile, difficulties arose in the Church, and Paul wrote a letter to them to correct their carnalities, and then he wrote a second letter to them, and in that second letter is the paragraph which I have in mind, with which I want to close. It is found in the sixth chapter of the second letter to the Corinthians, from the eleventh verse to the eighteenth. Professor Johnstone Ross once said to me that the second letter to the Corinthians is " the letter of Paul's broken heart." Paul's heart was breaking over the condition of the Corinthian Church. What was the matter with it ? Simply this, that the Church had caught the spirit of Corinth, and the evil things in Corinth had invaded the Corinthian Church.

Now in his second letter he said :

" Our mouth is open unto you, O Corinthians, our heart is enlarged. Ye are not straightened in us, but ye are straightened in your own affections. Now for a recompense in like kind (I speak as unto my children), be ye also enlarged. Be not unequally yoked with unbelievers ; for what fellowship have righteousness and iniquity ? or what communion hath light with darkness ?

" And what concord hath Christ with Belial ? or what portion hath a believer with an un-

believer ? And what agreement hath a temple of
God with idols ? for we are a temple of the living
God ; even as God said, I will dwell in them, and
walk in them ; and I will be their God, and they
shall be My people. Wherefore come ye out
from among them, and be ye separate, saith the
Lord, and touch no unclean thing ; and I will
receive you and will be to you a Father, and ye
shall be to Me sons and daughters, saith the Lord
Almighty."

It is interesting to note that in these words Paul
quoted sentences from Isaiah and Hosea, the prophets
contemporary to Judah and Israel.

Examine that paragraph. It opens with a negative
injunction. It closes with a positive injunction.
What is the negative injunction ? " Be not unequally
yoked with unbelievers." What is the closing injunction ? " Come ye out from among them, and be ye
separate, and touch no unclean thing."

Between these injunctions we find the apostolic
arguments for obedience. Notice these pulsating
questions. " What ? What ? What ? What ? four
times over. Each introduces a contrast. Observe the
contrasts—righteousness, iniquity ; light, darkness ;
Christ, Belial ; believer, unbeliever ; temple of God,
idols.

On one side he ranges the things for which the
Church stands : Righteousness, Light, Christ, a
believer, the Temple of God. On the other he names
the things which are opposed to the Church, and
which the Church is sent into the world to correct :
Iniquity, Darkness, Belial, Unbelief, Idolatry. Paul

is showing the antagonism between these things. In doing so, carefully observe the words he used. Every one of them is well chosen and carefully chosen. What *fellowship* between righteousness and iniquity ; what *communion* between light and darkness ; what *concord* between Christ and Belial ; between a believer and an unbeliever what *portion* ; between the temple of God and idols, what *agreement*.

What are these words, fellowship, communion, concord, portion, agreement, massed between these opposing things ? The first is fellowship, and the word means sharing. What sharing can there be ? What is there in iniquity that righteousness wants ? What is there in righteousness that iniquity desires ? They cannot share. His next word is the word communion. It means to have things in common. What is there in common between light and darkness ? There is nothing in common. They contradict each other eternally. Listen to the next. What concord between Christ and Belial ? Concord is a fine word with a Latin origin. The Greek word might be transliterated symphony. What symphony can there be between Christ and Belial ? A symphony is a sounding together in harmony. What sounding together can there be between Christ and Belial ? Between a believer and an unbeliever he asks what portion can there be ? The word portion means a lot, province, inheritance. How can they live together ? And then at last what agreement, which means common sentiment, what common sentiment can there be between the temple of God and idols ?

Paul did not answer the questions he asked. Reason gives the answer as the questions are asked. This being so, it is at once recognized that there is no disaster greater than that an hour should come when God has to say to His Israel, " Canaan ! " Those who were sent to cut the cancer out and establish a centre of health have caught the disease, have lost the power to heal and help humanity. Canaan is a terrible word when so used.

And that terrible word was spoken in Love. This is the love of God. What sickly, sentimental, stupid things we sometimes crystallize into apparently axiomatic affirmations. As, for instance, when we say, Love is blind. Love is never blind. Make no mistake. Love has keenest vision. There is a boy going wrong, and everybody can see it ; they know he is going wrong. And some one says every one sees it but his mother. She is blind. Again, make no mistake. His mother saw it long before you did. Eyes washed with tears always see most clearly, but " Love endureth all things, hopeth all things, believeth all things ; love never faileth." Love always sees. But that is not love which excuses the thing that is blasting the loved one. Love will make no terms with the things that blast humanity. It is because God is Love that He sees clearly the failure, makes no terms with it, and calls things by their right names. While the prophet, uttering the very message of God, was meditating the wonderful thing that Jacob became Israel, God says in effect, It is true ; but he has become Canaan. God's judgments are the judgments of truth and righteousness.

Our chief concern should be, that we who are the Israel of God, the people God-governed, should never become Canaan, a people humiliated by evil. We must make no terms with evil, no compromise with the things that are opposed to our Christ, no trafficking across the border line with Belial. We are to stand true and clean and pure and strong, in order that we may be a centre of healing and of blessing for the world.

XII

IDOLS AND GOD

HOSEA xiii. 2–xiv. 8

"Idols according to their understanding."—HOSEA xiii. 2.

"Ephraim shall say, What have I to do any more with idols ? I have answered and will regard Him ; I am like a green fir tree ; from me is Thy fruit found."—HOSEA xiv. 8.

THE first text is from the third address of Jehovah. After the second, the keynote of which was " Canaan," and a prophetic interpolation, describing Ephraim's sin, we come to this third speech of Jehovah. In its entirety it is a message of love, declaring the ultimate triumph of love, in spite of all the difficulties and sins of the people ; ending with that great challenge, " I will ransom them from the power of Sheol ; I will redeem them from death " ; and then those great words which Paul quoted, " O death, where are thy plagues ? O Sheol, where is thy destruction ? " ; and this declaration, " Repentance shall be hid from Mine eyes," which does not mean He will pay no attention to repentant souls, but that He has determined on the restoration of the people as they return to Him, and will not repent.

In the beginning of this message the nature of their sin is declared, " Idols according to their own under-

standing.'' This is a revelation of the religious action
which follows departure from God. In a previous
meditation (Hosea iv. 17) we dealt with the subject of
idols, and now touch upon it briefly only, considering
its cause, its course, and its curse.

The second text is taken from the final message of
Jehovah to Israel. In his last interpolation the
prophet had foretold the inevitable judgments of God
upon the sinning nation, and had appealed to the
nation to return to Jehovah. Then resuming the
Divine Message, his ministry ended on the high note
of hope as he foretold a way and a day of restoration
and realization. In that message there are two movements—the action of Jehovah, and the result.

Let us briefly then think first of idolatry ; its cause,
its course, and its curse.

What is the cause of idolatry ? Why have men
ever in the history of humanity made idols for themselves ? Idolatry is a false answer to the religious
call of human nature. The cause is to be found in the
clouding of the vision of God.

What does that mean ? Why should that issue in
idolatry ? Why have men made idols ? The answer
is self-evident. Humanity is so created that it has an
inherent necessity for God. Every man has his god.
Every human being is devoting the force of life to
something. Dr. Henry Van Dyke, in *The Ruling
Passion*, says that in every life worth writing about
there is a ruling passion. He goes on to suggest that
it may be music or art, business, family, home. He
declares that such ruling passion is the mainspring
of the life, and that if we are going to study any
personality, we are moving in a realm of mystery

until we have found it. The ruling passion is the
secret of a life. I have not quoted the exact words,
but the spirit of the paragraph, which is a very arresting one. I would personally delete three words from
the beginning of that quotation, " Worth writing
about." In every life there is a ruling passion. No
human being can any more live without that, than
a watch can run if the mainspring be taken out. That
is the cause of all idolatry.

Now mark the course of it. They make them, says
this word, " according to their own understanding."
When men have lost the vision of God, and have to
construct a god, they do it according to their own
understanding. They try to evolve within their own
thinking an idea of God. Take the illustration found
in the history of Israel, that is the northern kingdom,
to which Hosea was a messenger. What was the form
of their idolatry ? It had taken two forms from the
disruption of the kingdom. When Solomon died the
kingdom was rent in twain. Jeroboam became king
over the northern kingdom, and Rehoboam king of
the southern. Jeroboam, for political purposes, set
up a new centre of worship. He did not deny Jehovah,
but according to his understanding made a likeness
of Jehovah. That was the meaning of the calves.
That was the first movement in Israel's idolatries,
a false representation of God, according to their own
understanding.

When we reach the days of Ahab, that incarnation
of godlessness, we find that they were not worshipping
things intended to represent God, but had substituted
other gods for the one God. That was the second
phase : " Idols according to their own understanding."

The curse of idolatry is inherent in the process. When men make idols they make them like themselves, and the result is disastrous, This is set forth in Psalm cxv., in which the Singer describes such idols, and shows the result of worshipping them :

> " They have mouths, but they speak not ;
> Eyes have they, but they see not ;
> They have ears, but they hear not ;
> Noses have they, but they smell not ;
> They have hands, but they handle not ;
> Feet have they, but they walk not ;
> Neither speak they through their throat.
> They that make them shall be like unto them ;
> Yea, every one that trusteth in them."

This reveals the vicious circle. Men make idols like themselves, imperfect, polluted, debased, and then become more and more like the idols so created. Such is the curse of idolatry.

Now let us turn to our other text, and the message of hope with which the prophecy ends. In it we turn from idols to God.

Beginning at the fourth verse we hear the voice of God Himself ; and in the message there are two movements, one describing the action of Jehovah, and the other telling the results of that action. The first is revealed in the recurrence of the words " I will," and the second in the recurrence of the words " He shall " or " They shall."

Thus the action of God :

> " I will heal their backsliding, I will love them freely ; for Mine anger is turned away from him. I will be as the dew unto Israel."

Thus the results :

" He shall blossom as the lily, and cast forth his roots as Lebanon. His branches shall spread, and his beauty shall be as the olive-tree, and his smell as Lebanon. They that dwell under his shadow shall return ; they shall revive as the grain, and blossom as the vine ; the scent thereof shall be as the wine of Lebanon. Ephraim shall say, What have I to do any more with idols ? I have answered, and will regard Him ; I am like a green fir-tree ; from me is Thy fruit found."

Let us then survey the whole message, and then consider this final statement of what Ephraim has to say.

The first matter in the statement is that of the " I wills " of Jehovah. " I will heal their backsliding." In other words, I will cure them of their apostasy. Not, I will heal the wounds resulting from their backsliding. That is quite true, but it is secondary. I will cure the malady of their apostasy.

The question as to how God can do this is answered in the next affirmation : " I will love them freely." Freely means of My own will and My own heart, quite independently of them or of their deserts. I will not love them in response to their love. I will love them in spite of their rebellion. Reverently let me put it : I will love them because I cannot help loving them. That is God. And it is because of that deep thing in the nature of God that He first said, " I will heal their backsliding," I will cure the malady of their apostasy.

And then follows this arresting word : " I will be

as the dew unto Israel." That is the third time the figure of the dew has been employed by the prophet in the course of his prophesying. God, speaking to the same people, had said : " O Ephraim, what shall I do unto thee ? O Judah, what shall I do unto thee ? for your goodness is as a morning cloud, and as the dew that goeth early away." God's complaint against them was that their goodness was evanescent, was vanishing as the early dew. God had also employed it as a symbol of judgment : " Therefore they shall be as the morning cloud, and as the dew that passeth early away."

Now the word is used again. " I will be as the dew unto Israel." Here we must interpret the figure by the personality. In the earlier uses of the figure there were qualifying words ; " the *early* dew " ; " the dew that passeth early away." There is no qualifying word here. Here the figure must be interpreted by the timeless eternity of God. With Him it is always morning, or if not, then with Him there is dew at noontide, and dew in the evening. " I will be as the dew."

Then we turn to the description of results. Because God is as the dew to him, he shall blossom as the lily. The lily stands for beauty and purity. The nation under the fertilizing power of love created by the dew of the Divine presence, shall become characterized by the beauty and the purity of the lily.

Then with a fine and swift poetic movement, as though this figure of the lily breaks down a little, for the lily has little root ; it soon passes away ; " and cast forth his roots as Lebanon." Not only beauty, not only purity, but stability. Lebanon is the synonym for the cedar. The poetry runs on perfectly. The prophet saw the lily with its beauty and its purity. Ephraim shall blossom like that. Yes, but that is not all. Ephraim's roots shall be as the cedars of Lebanon.

Again the figure changes, " His branches shall spread, and his beauty shall be as the olive tree." The lily, the cedar, the olive ; the lily for beauty and purity ; the cedar for roots that spread far beneath, and touch the underground rivers ; and therefore with branches that spread out in magnificence ; and the olive, evergreen.

Mark the symbolism of it all. Beauty, purity, strength, fidelity ; and then look at the nation as it was, ugly, impure, and deformed, weak and vacillating, and withered with heat, and bearing no fruit. Jehovah said : " I will be as the dew unto Israel " ; and therefore there shall be the fulfilment of all the highest and the noblest.

Follow on. " They "—it is not " he " now ; it is not the instrument, it is not Israel, but " they that dwell under his shadow," they that pass under the influence of this restored nation, " shall return, they shall revive as the grain, and blossom as the vine " ; and then it is, that the " scent thereof shall be as the wine of Lebanon."

The fulfilment of all this is coming through Christ. This nation as an earthly people was rejected when Jesus said in Temple courts, " The Kingdom of God shall be taken away from you, and shall be given to a nation bringing forth the fruits thereof." Almost immediately afterwards, the Lord was alone with His own disciples, and He said, " I am the Vine, ye are the branches." Everything of beauty and of glory and of strength and of fruitfulness, is to be produced through Him, and those associated with Him as branches in the Vine.

All this leads us in proper sequence to the words of our second text. It records the words of Ephraim consequent upon the activity of God in love. "Ephraim shall say," Ephraim healed of backsliding, because of God's love ; and, because God is becoming the dew, Ephraim blossoming as the lily, casting out its roots like the cedar of Lebanon, like the olive tree, Ephraim is now speaking. " What have I to do any more with idols ? "—Ephraim has broken with idols. What brought it about ? What does bring about the break with idols whenever it takes place ? What is it that brings Dagon crashing to the ground ? What is it that sweeps idolatry out of the soul of a man, or of a nation, so that it says, or he says, " What have I to do any more with idols ? " Ephraim replies to our questions. " I have answered and will regard Him." That is the secret. I have responded to Him. I have seen and yielded.

But there is more ; " And will regard Him." That means continuous contemplation. Ephraim has broken with idols, because somehow he has seen God anew ; and seeing Him, has responded to Him, has yielded to Him, and has come to the point in life when he says, Henceforth this is to be my attitude ; I will regard Him. Because Ephraim has come to the time when he has answered, and has now assumed the attitude of perpetual and continuous watching of God, he says, What have I to do with idols ? Dr. Chalmers, of Scotland, coined the phrase, " The expulsive power of a new affection." What a phrase it is. " I have answered Him, and will regard Him." " What have I to do with idols ? " The cure of idolatry is the restored vision of God.

And yet there is something else to say, " I am like a green fir tree." Ephraim is using a figure of speech. It is a new one. He does not use the lily, he does not use the cedar of Lebanon, or the olive tree. Perhaps we should say that nobody knows certainly what tree is meant by that fir tree. Personally I think it was the cypress tree. At any rate, it was a tree the chief characteristics of which were permanent freshness, and fruitfulness.

And so the culminative and inclusive word. " From me is Thy fruit found." We recall the words of a previous meditation : " Israel is a luxuriant vine that putteth forth his fruit." That was the complaint against Israel ; a luxuriant vine, but not bringing forth the fruit God was looking for. Or as Isaiah had it, " I looked that it should bring forth grapes, and it brought forth wild grapes." The condemnation of the nation was that it was a luxuriant vine, but not bringing forth the fruit God was seeking, but bringing forth its own fruit. Now at last the nation says : " From me is Thy fruit found." Thus is revealed the contrast between the self-centred, the God-forgetting, and the idolatry-blasted people ; and the God-centred, the God-remembering, and the God-honouring people.

The prophecy of Hosea ends on a note of challenge :

" Who is wise, that he may understand these things ? prudent, that he may know them ? for the ways of Jehovah are right, and the just shall walk in them ; but transgressors shall fall therein."

Note the two words " wise " and " prudent." The Hebrew word translated " wise " means intelligent. But intelligence is not enough. Who is prudent ? Prudent means acting according to intelligence. Prudent means squaring conduct with conviction.

The man intelligent and prudent will come to certain convictions. Of these the first is that " the ways of Jehovah are right." That summarizes everything. That being so, it follows that the righteous walk in them ; and the wicked fall in them.

God's ways are straight and true, and we walk, or fall according to our relationship with those ways.

We may summarize our understanding of the teachings of Hosea. It declares that sin separates from God, and blinds us, so that we lose the vision of Him. It shows that idolatry results from the loss of the vision of God. It most clearly reveals the Heart and the Holiness of God. His love is eternal, but is never divorced from moral requirement.

We are living in fuller light than Hosea had. We see God as Hosea never saw Him. We see Him in Jesus. There seeing Him, we know, as never before, that He can make no terms with sin ; but we know that He stays at no sacrifice in order that He may heal our backsliding.

If we are guilty of idolatry, what will cure us ? The vision of Him, as He was seen in Jesus Christ.

> " Hast thou heard Him, seen Him, known Him ?
>   Is not thine a captured heart ?
>   Chief among ten thousand own Him,
>   Joyful choose the better part.

Idols once they won thee, charmed thee,
  Lovely things of time and sense ;
Gilded thus does sin disarm thee,
  Honeyed lest thou turn thee thence.

What has stript the seeming beauty
  From the idols of the earth ?
Not a sense of right or duty,
  But the sight of peerless worth.

Not the crushing of those idols,
  With its bitter void and smart ;
But the beaming of His beauty,
  The unveiling of His heart.

Who extinguishes their taper
  Till they hail the rising sun ?
Who discards the garb of winter
  Till the summer has begun ?

'Tis that look that melted Peter,
  'Tis that face that Stephen saw,
'Tis that heart that wept with Mary,
  Can alone from idols draw.

Draw and win and fill completely,
  Till the cup o'erflow the brim ;
What have we to do with idols
  Who have companied with Him ? "